Sex and Pornography Addictions

Addictions

ReferencePoint
Press®

San Diego, CA

Other books in the Compact Research Addictions set:

Gambling Addiction
Heroin Addiction
Internet and Social Media Addiction
Synthetic Drug Addiction

*For a complete list of titles please visit www.referencepointpress.com.

COMPACT *Research*

Sex and Pornography Addictions

Christine Wilcox

Addictions

ReferencePoint
Press®

San Diego, CA

© 2015 ReferencePoint Press, Inc.
Printed in the United States

For more information, contact:
ReferencePoint Press, Inc.
PO Box 27779
San Diego, CA 92198
www.ReferencePointPress.com

Picture credits:
Maury Aaseng: 32–34, 46–48, 60–62, 75–76
Tek Image/Science Photo Library: 12
Thinkstock Images: 18

LIBRARY OF CONGRESS CATALOGING-IN-PUBLICATION DATA

Wilcox, Christine.
 Sex and pornography addictions/by Christine Wilcox.
  pages cm.--(Compact research series)
 Includes bibliographical references.
 ISBN 978-1-60152-762-2 (hardback)--ISBN 1-60152-762-4 (hardback) 1. Sex addiction.
2. Pornography. I. Title.
 RC560.S43W54   2015
 616.85'833--dc23
                                                                                    2014032378

Contents

Foreword   6

Sex and Pornography Addictions at a Glance   8

Overview   10

What Is Sex Addiction?   21
    Primary Source Quotes   28
    Facts and Illustrations   31

What Is Pornography Addiction?   35
    Primary Source Quotes   42
    Facts and Illustrations   45

Can Sex and Pornography Addictions Be Overcome?   49
    Primary Source Quotes   56
    Facts and Illustrations   59

Are Sex and Pornography Really Addictive?   63
    Primary Source Quotes   71
    Facts and Illustrations   74

Key People and Advocacy Groups   78

Chronology   80

Related Organizations   82

For Further Research   86

Source Notes   88

List of Illustrations   91

Index   92

About the Author   96

Foreword

❝Where is the knowledge we have lost in information?❞

—T.S. Eliot, "The Rock."

As modern civilization continues to evolve, its ability to create, store, distribute, and access information expands exponentially. The explosion of information from all media continues to increase at a phenomenal rate. By 2020 some experts predict the worldwide information base will double every seventy-three days. While access to diverse sources of information and perspectives is paramount to any democratic society, information alone cannot help people gain knowledge and understanding. Information must be organized and presented clearly and succinctly in order to be understood. The challenge in the digital age becomes not the creation of information, but how best to sort, organize, enhance, and present information.

ReferencePoint Press developed the *Compact Research* series with this challenge of the information age in mind. More than any other subject area today, researching current issues can yield vast, diverse, and unqualified information that can be intimidating and overwhelming for even the most advanced and motivated researcher. The *Compact Research* series offers a compact, relevant, intelligent, and conveniently organized collection of information covering a variety of current topics ranging from illegal immigration and deforestation to diseases such as anorexia and meningitis.

The series focuses on three types of information: objective single-author narratives, opinion-based primary source quotations, and facts and statistics. The clearly written objective narratives provide context and reliable background information. Primary source quotes are carefully selected and cited, exposing the reader to differing points of view, and facts and statistics sections aid the reader in evaluating perspectives. Presenting these key types of information creates a richer, more balanced learning experience.

For better understanding and convenience, the series enhances information by organizing it into narrower topics and adding design features that make it easy for a reader to identify desired content. For example, in *Compact Research: Illegal Immigration*, a chapter covering the economic impact of illegal immigration has an objective narrative explaining the various ways the economy is impacted, a balanced section of numerous primary source quotes on the topic, followed by facts and full-color illustrations to encourage evaluation of contrasting perspectives.

The ancient Roman philosopher Lucius Annaeus Seneca wrote, "It is quality rather than quantity that matters." More than just a collection of content, the *Compact Research* series is simply committed to creating, finding, organizing, and presenting the most relevant and appropriate amount of information on a current topic in a user-friendly style that invites, intrigues, and fosters understanding.

Sex and Pornography Addictions at a Glance

Sex Addiction Defined

Sex addiction is a pattern of unwanted sexual behavior that is acted out despite increasingly negative effects and attempts to stop.

Causes of Sex Addiction

Experts theorize that sex addiction is caused by childhood trauma and abuse. The trauma causes an attachment disorder, which prevents an individual from achieving intimacy with others.

Pornography Addiction Defined

Pornography addiction is a compulsion to spend excessive amounts of time viewing or masturbating to pornographic images despite increasingly negative effects and attempts to stop.

Causes of Pornography Addiction

While some pornography addicts have a history of childhood trauma, most become addicted to Internet pornography because of opportunity: Internet porn is easy to access, inexpensive, and anonymous.

Prevalence

Experts estimate that between 3 and 8 percent of the US population—between 9 million and 25 million people—are addicted to sex or pornography.

Accompanying Disorders

Almost all sex addicts have a personality disorder such as narcissistic personality disorder or a mood disorder such as depression. Other addictions, including alcoholism, are also common among sex and pornography addicts.

Possible Harms

Sex addiction puts individuals at higher risk of assault, STDs, and unwanted pregnancy. Pornography addiction is reported to cause sexual dysfunction. Both addictions can cause substantial harm to employment or relationships.

Pornography and Teens

Pornography may interfere with normal sexual development, causing an inability to become aroused by real-life encounters. Pornography may also give young people unrealistic expectations about normal sexuality.

Treatment Options

Sex and pornography addictions may be treated by individual therapy, in rehabilitation centers, through 12-step programs, or through online self-help groups.

Scientific Proof

There is no scientific proof that sex or pornography has the ability to be physically addictive like drugs or alcohol. Many believe that people label themselves as "addicts" to avoid taking responsibility for their actions.

Overview

66People who struggle with sex addiction have been taken over by their sexual appetites. Rather than being their master, they have become their slave.99

—Paula Hall, a sex addiction therapist and the founder of The Hall Recovery Course.

66I just don't see the value of the 'sex addiction' diagnosis. It assumes that people who FEEL out of control ARE out of control.99

—Marty Klein, a sex therapist and international lecturer on sexuality and public policy.

In 1987 Neil Melincovich was on his way to pick up his girlfriend from the airport when he felt compelled to detour long enough to have sex with a prostitute—the fourth woman he had had sex with in the past few days. Afterward, he found the prostitute's blood on his mouth. Even though it was the height of the AIDS epidemic in America, Melincovich did not tell his girlfriend about the incident and had unprotected sex with her as soon as they returned home.

Melincovich is one of the millions of Americans who suffer from sex addiction. He now runs a chapter of Sex Addicts Anonymous (SAA), a 12-step program founded in the late 1970s and modeled after Alcoholics Anonymous. Other sex addicts find help at treatment centers or in outpatient addiction therapy. Treatment can be expensive. It is almost never covered by insurance because sex addiction is not recognized by the *Diagnostic and Statistical Manual of Mental Disorders (DSM)*, the manual that mental health professionals use to diagnose illnesses. In fact, many health professionals do not believe that sex addiction is a disorder at all. As sex therapist Marty Klein explains, "When a lot of people who label themselves as sex addicts or porn addicts say, 'I'm out of control,' what they really mean is 'You know, it would be really uncomfortable to make different decisions about sex than the ones that I'm making. When I'm lonely it would be really uncomfortable to not look at porn.'"[1]

Despite the criticism, countless people have had their lives ruined by their inability to rein in their sexual excesses without outside help. As scientists are trying to determine whether out-of-control sexual behavior is just an extreme version of normal sexuality or a brain disease like alcoholism, addicts like Melincovich still struggle with their compulsions. "I'm kind of a work in progress," he says. "I'm still trying to define a healthy sexuality that works for me."[2]

What Is Sex Addiction?

Sex addiction does not have a single authoritative definition, but most definitions are based on the criteria for substance addiction. The Society for the Advancement of Sexual Health (SASH) defines sex addiction as "a persistent and escalating pattern or patterns of sexual behaviors acted out despite increasingly negative consequences to self or others."[3] In general, sex addicts are characterized by their inability to stop thinking about, pursuing, or engaging in sexual activity, despite significant negative consequences to their careers, their relationships, or their emotional or physical health. Sex addicts often masturbate compulsively, have brief relationships, frequent strip clubs or hire prostitutes, have risky sexual encounters, and seek out sexual experiences without considering the consequences. Because sex addiction is considered a behavioral or process addiction, addicts often spend much more time creating and engaging in rituals around the pursuit of sex than actually having sex.

> **Countless people have had their lives ruined by their inability to rein in their sexual excesses without outside help.**

While sex addicts usually have strong sex drives, once the process of addiction begins, the enjoyment they get out of orgasm can diminish

Like people who become addicted to heroin (pictured) or other drugs, people who experience sex addiction develop a need that must be satisfied just to feel normal. They are often seeking an escape from emotional pain rather than pleasure.

significantly. As David Linden, professor of neuroscience at the Johns Hopkins University School of Medicine, explains, "If you are a sex addict, just like a heroin addict, you have undergone that transformation, from liking to wanting. You are at the point where you are having sex not because you are deriving great pleasure from it, but because you need to do that just to fall asleep at night and wake up in the morning and face the day and not have withdrawal symptoms."[4] Like substance addicts, sex addicts often complain that they feel normal only immediately after their sexual "fix." Their addiction is no longer a pursuit of pleasure but an escape from emotional pain.

Problems with Intimacy

Sex addiction is sometimes referred to as an intimacy disorder. A sex addict's personal relationships are often characterized by a lack of emotional intimacy or connectedness. Because sex addicts often have difficulty achieving intimacy with their partners, they do not receive the emotional support intimate relationships provide. Instead, they are driven to use sexual rituals and orgasm to regulate mood and combat stress and anxiety. According to Robert Weiss, the founder of the Sexual Recovery Institute, sex addiction "is defined by repetitive patterns of sexual behavior utilized to self-medicate and/or stabilize emotional distress."[5]

> **Sex addicts . . . are driven to use sexual rituals and orgasm to regulate mood and combat stress and anxiety.**

A sex addict's problem with intimacy almost always has its roots in childhood. Studies have shown that up to 97 percent of all sex addicts suffered either physical, sexual, or emotional abuse in childhood. It is also common for sex addicts to have personality disorders (such as narcissistic personality disorder), mental disorders (such as bipolar disorder), or other addictions. This is one reason for a great deal of the controversy in the medical community about whether sex addiction should be considered a symptom of another disorder or should be treated as a primary addiction.

What Is Pornography Addiction?

Nineteen-year-old Calum masturbates fifteen times or more a day. "Every bit of spare time I have in the day is spent watching porn,"[6] he tells Martin Daubney, who interviewed him for the documentary *Porn on the Brain*. Calum feels compelled to watch Internet pornography as much as possible.

Even when he has clearly overdone it and his climaxes are painful, he is still driven to act on his urges. But Calum does not have many of the characteristics of a sex addict—he actually prefers masturbating to having sex, and he often chooses porn over sexual encounters with attractive women. He is one of the millions of young people who grew up with Internet pornography. Now that he is addicted, he has no idea of how to stop.

Most experts define pornography addiction as the compulsive, repeated use of pornographic material despite negative consequences. Even though pornography addiction is a type of sex addiction, and many sex addicts compulsively masturbate to pornography as one of the many outlets for their addiction, a subset of people who use pornography compulsively do not have the typical profile of the sex addict. They do not have a history of significant childhood abuse, nor do they have any of the underlying mental or personality disorders common to sex addicts. They enjoy healthy relationships with others—at least until their pornography addiction takes over their lives. Still, their pornography use progresses from habit to compulsion to addiction. It is these individuals who usually are referred to as pornography addicts by addiction experts.

Pornography addicts develop a form of tolerance to the pornography they view. They require more and more graphic and shocking images to reach orgasm. This is one reason that addicts spend so much time watching porn—part of their ritual can be a lengthy search for the right image or video. Some addicts further ritualize the process by accumulating and organizing vast collections of pornography. They also can find themselves becoming aroused by images, behaviors, and situations that violate their personal values. One compulsive pornography user describes his experience as a sophomore in high school: "If a threesome was kinky last week, then I'd need something wilder this week. To reach climax, I had to find that same toxic mix of shame and lust. . . . I felt ashamed about the type of porn that I was watching."[7]

Signs of Sex and Pornography Addictions

No screening tests for sex and pornography addictions have been accepted by the American Psychological Association (APA). Most clinicians use either a diagnostic tool developed in the 1980s called the Sexual Addiction Screening Test (SAST) or one of the many diagnostic tools that are based on the *DSM*'s diagnostic criteria for substance use disorder.

Signs and symptoms usually fall under one of several categories, some of which are similar to common signs of drug addiction. Among these are tolerance and withdrawal.

In drug addiction, tolerance refers to the way the body physically adjusts to addictive substances so that more is needed to achieve the same effect. In sex and pornography addictions, tolerance usually refers to the way addicts typically need more and more intensity to reach orgasm or have a satisfying sexual encounter. This is often referred to as escalation. Sex addicts are often compelled to engage in sex that is progressively riskier, more intense, or more shocking. Pornography addicts often need to view images that are more shocking or taboo in order to achieve orgasm.

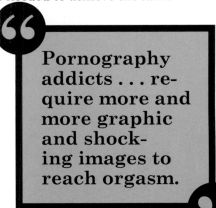

> **Pornography addicts . . . require more and more graphic and shocking images to reach orgasm.**

In drug addiction, withdrawal describes the adjustment period a person's body goes through when he or she stops taking an addictive substance. Chemical withdrawal symptoms can be extremely painful and, in the case of alcohol withdrawal (also known as delirium tremens, or the DTs), can even be fatal. Withdrawal from sex or pornography addiction is milder. Reported withdrawal symptoms include headaches, anxiety, anger, sweating, depression, insomnia, loss of energy, hypersensitivity, chills, heart palpitations, and intense cravings.

Other Signs of Addiction

If the object of addiction has salience, it has become the focus of an individual's thinking process. Sex addicts will spend considerable time and energy thinking about sex, pursuing sex partners, or engaging in rituals that lead up to sexual encounters (dressing, grooming, etc.). Pornography addicts will spend increasing amounts of time viewing pornography or arranging their schedules so they can view pornography. Addicts often neglect their jobs, their families, or other important aspects of their lives.

For both sex and pornography addicts, signs of the loss of control over the addiction include being unable to moderate or stop the activity despite harm to themselves, their families, or others—even if the addict has a strong desire to do so. For instance, sex addicts will often risk their health by having unprotected sex with strangers. Pornography addicts will access pornography at work, even though it puts their job at risk.

Some practitioners believe that warning signs of sex and pornography addictions include having an interest or engaging in sexual practices that are not part of a traditional, monogamous, committed relationship. Specifically, some practitioners believe that using prostitutes, having multiple relationships at once, being aroused by kink (such as cross-dressing, role-playing, etc.), or frequenting strip or sex clubs are signs of sex addiction. Being secretive about one's sexual practices is also said to be a sign of addiction. These criteria have come under criticism because they reflect cultural and religious values, not psychological dysfunction.

Distress and Inability to Stop

Many people assume that a person who is promiscuous, who masturbates multiple times a day, or who engages in unusual sexual practices must be a sex addict. Despite the rash of celebrities who go into treatment for sex addiction after they are caught cheating on their spouses, sex addiction has nothing to do with having a strong sex drive, liking sex, or being promiscuous. Most experts believe that a diagnosis of sex addiction can only be made if a person's sexual behavior causes him or her significant distress. As one recovering sex addict explains, "It's not the sexual behavior in itself that defines a sex addict . . . it's how it makes you feel afterwards: the powerlessness, the obsession, the guilt and the shame."[8] For instance, a person who enjoys watching pornography for several hours a day, or who prefers to have one-night stands rather than be in a committed relationship, is not a pornography or sex addict—unless he or she is distressed by the behavior and cannot stop it.

> Young people who are frequently aroused and feel compelled to have sex or masturbate multiple times a day are not sex addicts.

Most experts say that sex addiction should not be confused with sexual fetishes such as sadomasochism. While sex addicts often do engage in alternative or unusual sexual practices (which is why some experts consider them to be a warning sign of sexual addiction), the practices themselves do not define the addiction. Many people engage in fetishistic behavior without suffering any distress. And those who do feel distress are often simply reacting to the social stigma against these behaviors. People who experience unwanted homosexual urges also are not sex addicts even if they feel compelled to act on those urges. As Weiss explains, "Sexual addiction is not in any way defined by what or who an individual finds arousing."[9]

Finally, and important to note, is that teenagers who are going through puberty—especially teen males—normally have a strong sex drive. Human sexuality experts stress that young people who are frequently aroused and feel compelled to have sex or masturbate multiple times a day are not sex addicts. However, some addiction experts claim that young people who use pornography excessively do run the risk of developing pornography addiction, which can cause sexual dysfunction and other problems.

Prevalence of Sex and Pornography Addiction

Experts estimate that between 3 and 8 percent of the US population—or between 9 million and 25 million people—are addicted to sex or pornography. Some experts estimate that 90 percent of all sex addicts are male. Others estimate that about two-thirds are male and one-third are female. One reason that it is difficult to know for sure is that women are less likely to seek help for sex or pornography addiction than are men. Weiss estimates that only 8 to 12 percent of those seeking treatment are female but that many more women may be suffering from the disorder.

No reliable statistics exist on whether sex and pornography addictions have increased or decreased over time. However, the increase of sex addiction treatment options over the last decade suggests either an increase in addiction or an increase in knowledge—possibly fueled by publicity about the disorder. In 2011 over fifteen hundred psychologists specializing in sex addiction were practicing in the United States, up from about one hundred in 2001.

Types of Sexual Addiction

Sex addiction therapists sometimes find it useful to characterize a sex addict by the type of sexual activity he or she engages in. Psychologist Patrick J. Carnes, who developed the modern theory of sex addiction in

Pornography addiction may be rising thanks to easy access on the Internet. Viewers on Internet porn sites can also remain anonymous.

the 1980s, identified ten types of sex addiction in his early research. For instance, he found that some sex addicts act out with anonymous sex, such as one-night stands or sex with prostitutes. Others prefer intrusive sex, such as rubbing up against another person in a sexual way without their permission.

Pornography addiction and love addiction are often talked about separately from sex addiction, though they are types of sexual addiction. Sexual anorexia is a term that refers to being repelled by sex, and Carnes claimed it was sometimes part of the addiction cycle. Hypersexual disorder is a term that essentially means sex addiction. The medical community tends to use the term hypersexual disorder because it does not emphasize the addictive qualities of sex, which have not been proved.

Can Sex and Pornography Addiction Be Overcome?

Some experts believe that sex and pornography addiction can be overcome; others say that sexual addictions are lifelong disorders and that addicts must remain vigilant for life against the return of their addictions. Twelve-step programs are the most common form of treatment for sex addiction. These programs modify the twelve steps of Alcoholics Anonymous to fit sexual activities. For instance, the concept of sexual sobriety does not involve complete abstinence from sex—though it often requires that the addict stop masturbating. Instead, sexual sobriety means engaging only in sexual practices that support healthy sexual expression. According to Sexaholics Anonymous (SA), "True sobriety includes progressive victory over lust."[10] SA considers any sex outside of a committed relationship to be progressively addictive and destructive.

Other organizations treat sex and pornography addiction from a Christian perspective. The American Association of Christian Counselors offers a certificate training program in treating sexual addiction, and Christian-based treatment programs often host conferences and seminars for Christians who are concerned about their own or a loved one's sex addiction or, more commonly, use of pornography. Christian-based programs equate sexual addiction with sin, and prayer is a part of treatment. Like 12-step programs, they define healthy sex as sex within a committed relationship.

> **Sexual sobriety means engaging only in sexual practices that support healthy sexual expression.**

Treatment is also available in rehabilitation centers across the country. Most of these centers primarily treat substance addictions, but they have expanded their programs to meet the growing demand for sexual addiction treatment.

Online or do-it-yourself treatment options are also becoming popular. One innovative option is NoFap, a group started on the social media site Reddit that is made up of people who wish to quit masturbating (or "fapping"). Currently, NoFap has over one hundred thousand members, many of whom claim that abstaining from masturbation has improved their lives dramatically.

Are Sex and Pornography Really Addictive?

There is a great deal of controversy about whether natural activities like sexual arousal and orgasm can be addictive. In the medical community addiction has a very specific meaning; addictive substances are made up of powerful chemicals that change the brain to such an extent that addiction is considered by most doctors to be a disease of the brain. Calling sex an addictive activity implies that people can be addicted to their own brain chemicals, which many doctors do not believe is possible. Also, no scientific proof backs up the claims of sexual addiction specialists, though this is largely due to a lack of interest in funding research.

Klein believes that many sex addicts are simply narcissistic people. "It's someone who is unhappy with the consequences of their sexual choices," Klein says, "but who finds it too emotionally painful to make different choices."[11] Klein points out that the sex addiction movement did not arise out of the sex therapy field. Carnes, who coined the phrase "sex addiction" in 1983 in his book *Out of the Shadows*, has a background in counselor education and organizational development, not human sexuality. "Almost thirty years after its invention by Carnes," Klein writes, "'sex addiction' is still not a popular concept in the fields of sex therapy, sex education, or sex research."[12]

> " Calling sex an addictive activity implies that people can be addicted to their own brain chemicals, which many doctors do not believe is possible. "

There are signs that sex addiction—along with other behavioral addictions like Internet addiction—will soon be accepted by the APA as valid disorders. In 2013 a behavioral addiction—gambling disorder—was included in the *DSM* for the first time. And in 2014, a small study found similarities in the brains of pornography addicts and drug addicts. While some people who claim to be sex addicts are simply trying to excuse their infidelity, science may soon prove that sex and pornography have the potential to be just as addictive as drugs and alcohol.

What Is Sex Addiction?

66It's all about chasing that emotional high: losing your-self in image after image, prostitute after prostitute, affair after affair. [Sex addicts] end up losing relation-ships, getting diseases, and losing jobs.99

—Robert Weiss, a sex addiction expert and the founder of the Sexual Recovery Institute.

66A love addict may feel that true love will solve everything.99

—Moushumi Ghose, a sex therapist in Los Angeles, California.

Sex addiction is poorly understood by the medical community, in part because so few formal studies have been done on the disorder. Researchers find it difficult to get funding for studies, and surveys about sex are often inaccurate. Most of what experts know about sex addiction is anecdotal, which means it is based on the reported experiences of addicts and clinicians rather than on scientific research. Still, surveys and anecdotal information have revealed quite a bit about the causes of sex addiction and the behavior of addicts.

Does Childhood Trauma Cause Sex Addiction?

The overwhelming majority of people who have been diagnosed with sex addiction have suffered childhood trauma. From 1985 to 2003, Patrick J. Carnes conducted a series of studies of 650 sex addicts and found that 72 percent reported childhood physical abuse, 81 percent reported childhood sexual abuse, and 97 percent reported childhood emotional abuse.

Seventy-seven percent described their families as rigid, dogmatic, and inflexible, and 87 percent said their families were detached, uninvolved, and emotionally absent. "Thus, [sex addicts] came from environments in which failure to bond was the norm,"[13] Carnes writes.

One theory about why childhood trauma causes sex addiction is that it causes a lifelong hypersensitivity to stress and danger. According to sex addiction expert Paula Hall, "Sexual behavior may become a way for a trauma sufferer to numb feelings of . . . hyperactivity, obsessive thinking, rage and panic and also alleviate feelings of disassociation, numbness, depression and exhaustion."[14]

Attachment Disorders

Children who fail to bond with their caretakers often develop what is known as an attachment disorder, which causes them to be unable to create emotional bonds with others in later life. They also never learn to regulate their emotions; therefore, they seek out substances or behaviors to ease their discomfort. Attachment disorders are common in sex addicts. As sex addiction therapist Alexandra Katehakis explains, "Because [sex addicts] didn't get the appropriate input and modeling for how to seek and receive comfort from the adults in their lives, they turn to substances or behaviors that will give them temporary relief from their own internal deregulation. Over time, the habituated use of sex or obsessive love, become patterned behaviors that are difficult to stop."[15]

> Sex addicts . . . often believe that sex is their most important emotional need—the only thing that can bring them comfort and a sense of well-being.

Three types of attachment disorder patterns are commonly found in sex addicts. The anxious-avoidant type tends to avoid intimacy. This type usually seeks out sexual encounters that do not include emotion, such as sex with prostitutes. The anxious-ambivalent type tends to crave intimacy one minute and distance the next. This type often seeks sex outside of his or her primary relationships in an effort to avoid both commitment and abandonment at the same time. Finally, the disorganized type often acts out of fear, afraid of being both smothered and abandoned. This type tends to binge on sexual encounters, moving quickly from partner to partner in a destructive pattern.

Because of their attachment disorders, most sex addicts avoid emotional intimacy. They tend to either be isolated or isolate themselves, and many have created environments in which they lack accountability. They often believe that sex is their most important emotional need—the only thing that can bring them comfort and a sense of well-being.

Self-Soothing with Sex

According to psychologist and addiction expert Stanton Peele, all addicts use their addictions to self-soothe. Peele writes, "Addiction is the search for emotional satisfaction—for a sense of security, a sense of being loved, even a sense of control over life."[16] This concept is at the foundation of the theory that people who use sex compulsively are actually addicted to sex. Whether a sex addict has a history of childhood trauma, an attachment disorder, or both, he or she becomes dependent on the brain chemicals produced by sexual behavior to deal with the stresses of life.

Robert Weiss is one of the most vocal proponents of the concept that compulsive sexual behavior is an addiction rather than a compulsive disorder or a character defect. He says that sex addicts "are addicted to the neurochemical and dissociative high produced by their intense sexual fantasy life and ritualistic behavior."[17] In other words, the drug of choice for sex addicts is their own brain chemistry.

Personality Disorders

Researchers have found that sex addicts usually have symptoms of one of the ten personality disorders officially recognized by the APA. People with personality disorders think and behave in ways that can cause dysfunction—especially in their relationships with others. In a 2013 study published in *Sexual Addiction & Compulsivity*, researchers surveyed 132 men who were seeking help for sexual addiction and found that 92 percent of them exhibited symptoms of a personality disorder.

Personality disorders that often appear in sex addicts are the narcissistic type, the borderline type, and the dependent type. Narcissistic personalities have a high opinion of themselves, a need for admiration, and little awareness of the feelings of others. Borderline personalities are characterized by impulsivity and victimization; they have trouble forming long-lasting attachments and seem to be addicted to the emotional drama that can occur in romantic and sexual relationships. Dependent personality types have a need to be cared for and a fear of abandonment. People with this type of personality disorder are often said to have a love addiction rather than a sex addiction because they confuse sex and love.

> **Some experts believe that sex addiction . . . should be treated as a symptom, not a primary disease.**

Some experts believe that sex addiction is really a by-product of a personality disorder or of a mental illness like bipolar disorder and should be treated as a symptom, not a primary disease. Others believe that sex addiction is the primary disorder, and people are erroneously diagnosed with a personality or mental disorder instead of an addiction. According to Gary Wilson, host of the website Your Brain On Porn, "[Sex] addiction's symptoms are easily mistaken for ADHD, social anxiety, depression, performance anxiety, and a host of others."[18]

The Cycle of Addiction

Roger, who is married and has two young children, was caught in a pattern of sexual addiction. When the stress at work got overwhelming, the only way he could relax was by fantasizing about sex—in particular, about sex with his boss's assistant. He started checking out online dating sites and chat rooms, striking up intense correspondences with several women at once, and arranging dates. He then went on a sexual binge, sleeping with as many women as he could. Shortly afterward he became disgusted by his behavior and swore off other women. A few weeks later, the cycle began again.

The pattern of sex addiction usually follows a predictable course that is similar to the pattern of other types of addiction. Weiss identifies six stages of the sexual addiction cycle:

1. *Onset of strong emotions*: Because sex addicts have not learned how to self-soothe, they are especially vulnerable to strong emotions like anger or fear. Their sexual acting out can be triggered by conflict, criticism, disappointment, worry, or any negative emotion. In Roger's case, stress at work triggered his addiction cycle.

2. *Fantasy*: The pain caused by the triggering event compels sex addicts to fantasize about getting their fix, or sexually acting out. When in a state of emotional pain any sexual cue can push the addict toward fantasy. Roger fantasized about a woman he saw every day—his boss's assistant.

> **While immersed in ritual, addicts are completely distracted from their pain and riding an emotional high.**

3. *Ritual*: The ritual stage is when sex addicts begin to take action. Their method of pursuing sex is usually the same each time. In Roger's case he looked for sex partners online. While immersed in ritual, addicts are completely distracted from their pain and riding an emotional high—sometimes called "being in the bubble."

4. *Acting Out*: This is the sexual binge, which can take many forms. Many sex addicts act out compulsively, but they no longer get much pleasure from sexual acts or climax. Acting out does not have to be having intercourse—it can be any kind of sexual behavior.

5. *Release*: After acting out, addicts sometimes feel a sense of relaxation from the release of tension. However, relaxation is often quickly replaced by regret, shame, and despair, which heighten their feelings of low self-worth. Addicts commonly make promises to themselves or others that they will not repeat the behavior again.

6. *Anxiety/Depression*: Addicts return to their baseline state of anxiety and depression over their behavior. These emotions leave them vulnerable to another triggering event, and the cycle begins again.

The Bubble

According to Weiss, "Sex addiction is not about sex or orgasm. It is about the search for sex and desire for orgasm. It's a process addiction."[19] The process that sex addicts are addicted to occurs in the fantasy and ritual stage, when sex is pursued. During this stage sex addicts experience a rush or high as they anticipate and work toward achieving their goal. They use this high to avoid feelings of depression, anxiety, or stress—in other words, to forget their problems.

This heightened state is commonly referred to by addicts as being in "the bubble" or "the trance," or being "on the hunt." While in the bubble sex addicts focus intensely on getting what they desire to the exclusion of everything else. Rituals help a sex addict enter the bubble. For instance, some addicts develop rituals around hiring a prostitute. They may dress in a certain way, stop at a particular ATM to withdraw cash, and drive to a particular neighborhood. While performing the ritual, the addict's focus is entirely on the anticipation of having sex. "When you're in that trance state, you just don't care about anything," explains Sarah, a recovering sex addict. "You might end up spending too much money, abandoning your kids, or not coming home for three days."[20] The bubble metaphor is apt because immediately after orgasm the bubble pops, and the addict comes back to reality—often immediately filled with shame and regret.

Love Addiction

Sue is having an affair with Rick—the latest in a long line of men she has risked her marriage to be with. In her memoir she writes, "These men see me just as an object, a body. They are men incapable of love—even though I endlessly, addictively, try to convince myself that sex at noon for an hour with a married man has to be the real thing, must be love." Sue's therapist explains that Sue has confused sex with love because her father sexually abused her. She understands this, yet she cannot resist the lure of the intensity of her relationship with Rick. "Only when my body is desired do I feel beautiful, powerful, loved."[21]

> "Love addicts seek the rush or high that goes along with the pursuit of romantic relationships."

Sue has a love addiction. Love addiction is a type of sex addiction that is more common in females. Love addicts seek the rush or high that goes along with the pursuit of romantic relationships, which they use to mask their own emotional pain. They also tend to confuse sex with love and to mistake a casual sexual relationship for a romantically intense one.

For a love addict, being in a relationship creates feelings of safety, happiness, and optimism. Because love addicts crave the security of a relationship, they will often put their partners' needs ahead of their own, which makes them vulnerable to abuse. They also frequently have issues with self-esteem. "Love addicts often are afraid of being alone, and don't like their own company," explains sex addiction therapist Moushumi Ghose. "Some may jump from one relationship to another in search of that excitement, while others stay in their current situation despite feelings of dissatisfaction."[22]

The Consequences of Sex Addiction

"My life pretty much crashed and burned because of my sex addiction," explains Ben, a fifty-four-year-old recovering sex addict. "I lost my marriage, my job, my family, most of my money; and now I'm having to face up to the pain I caused a lot of people."[23] Sex addicts often cause significant harm to their health, well-being, and relationships. The risky sexual behavior sex addicts engage in puts them at higher risk of unwanted pregnancy and contracting sexually transmitted diseases. And having sex with strangers puts both genders at risk of robbery, rape, and assault. However, the compulsion can be so powerful that many sex addicts ignore these dangers. For instance, Valerie, a sex addict who serially cheated on both of her husbands, could not stop even when her lover's wife aimed a shotgun at her head. It took an unsuccessful suicide attempt to convince her that she needed help.

> "Because relationships are marked by lies, betrayal, and neglect, addicts often feel intense shame about the harm they do to others.

Perhaps the most harmful aspect of sex addiction is the toxic level of shame it creates in the addict. Because relationships are marked by lies, betrayal, and neglect, addicts often feel intense shame about the harm they do to others. They also find themselves doing things that they believe are wrong. Because of this, they often think they are fundamentally bad people. According to Hall, "In every case that I have worked with, sex addiction contradicts the personal value system of the individual, leaving them feeling ashamed and out of control."[24] Because this shame is often too intense for the addict to handle, it triggers more sexual acting out, trapping the addict in the cycle of addiction.

What Is Sex Addiction?

66 Having risky sex without protection, paying for sex and taking the chance of getting arrested, and doing this despite the impact to you and your family can point to addictive behaviors rather than just liking sex. 99

—Janie Lacy, "How Do You Know When Sex Has Become an Addiction?," GoodTherapy.org, September 5, 2012. www.goodtherapy.org.

Lacy is a sex therapist and licensed mental health counselor in Maitland, Florida.

66 This diagnosis [sex addiction] poses a real risk of stigma and shame to innocent people, simply because their sexual behaviors do not fit what is defined as the social norm. 99

—David J. Ley, *The Myth of Sex Addiction*, Kindle edition. Lanham, MD: Rowman & Littlefield, 2012.

Ley is a clinical psychologist in Albuquerque, New Mexico.

Bracketed quotes indicate conflicting positions.

* Editor's Note: While the definition of a primary source can be narrowly or broadly defined, for the purposes of Compact Research, a primary source consists of: 1) results of original research presented by an organization or researcher; 2) eyewitness accounts of events, personal experience, or work experience; 3) first-person editorials offering pundits' opinions; 4) government officials presenting political plans and/or policies; 5) representatives of organizations presenting testimony or policy.

> ❝ Sex addicts stimulate sexual arousal and emotional intensity to become euphoric or 'numb-out,' much like substance addicts use cocaine or alcohol. ❞

—Connie A. Lofgreen, *The Storm of Sex Addiction: Rescue and Recovery*, Kindle edition. Omaha, NE: Starpro, 2012.

Lofgreen is a certified sex addiction therapist and the director of STARPRO, an outpatient sexual treatment and recovery program.

> ❝ For the insecurely attached individual, the [brain] may no longer produce sufficient dopamine. . . . An external source may become increasingly relied upon for something that the brain has not learnt to manufacture for itself. ❞

—Paula Hall, "A Biopsychosocial View of Sex Addiction," *Sexual and Relationship Therapy*, vol. 26, no. 3, August 2011, p. 221.

Hall is a sex addiction therapist and founder of The Hall Recovery Course.

> ❝ Love addiction can take over and cause people to make bad choices, fail to see red flags, and continue down a path with someone despite the obvious. ❞

—Moushumi Ghose, "Addicted to Love: Drawn to the Rush of Romance," GoodTherapy.org, November 2, 2012. www.goodtherapy.org.

Ghose is a sex therapist in Los Angeles, California.

> ❝ Sexual addiction is the disease of isolation! Living in shame, trying to get by on your own, withdrawing to the familiar routines when the pain comes are all dangers that keep someone bound and defeated. ❞

—Janie Lacy, "Three Things You Can Do in Overcoming Sex Addiction," GoodTherapy.org, March 14, 2011. www.goodtherapy.org.

Lacy is a sex therapist and licensed mental health counselor in Maitland, Florida.

❝[Fifty-two]" percent of my [sex addiction] patients come in suicidal.❞

—Patrick J. Carnes, interviewed by Joe Polish, "Sexual Addiction Interview with Dr. Patrick Carnes," Pine Grove Behavioral Health and Addiction Services, March 13, 2014. www.pinegrovetreatment.com.

Carnes is a psychologist who is widely regarded as the father of sexual addiction research.

❝Many of the addicts I've worked with do not get sexual pleasure from what they're doing and it does not satiate their [sex] drive.❞

—Paula Hall, *Understanding and Treating Sex Addiction*, Kindle edition. New York: Routledge, 2013.

Hall is a sex addiction therapist and founder of The Hall Recovery Course.

Facts and Illustrations

What Is Sex Addiction?

- Patrick Carnes, one of the nation's leading experts on sex addiction, estimates that **5 to 8 percent** of Americans, or **between 15 million and 25 million** people, are sex addicts.

- Patrick Carnes estimates that about **62.5 percent** of all American sex addicts are male, and about **37.5 percent** are female.

- Dr. Robert Weiss, founder of the Sexual Recovery Institute, estimates that only **8 to 12 percent** of those seeking treatment for sex addiction are female.

- *Satyriasis* and *nymphomania* are clinical terms for male and female sex addiction that are no longer widely used in the United States.

- People with bipolar disorder sometimes exhibit symptoms of sex addiction during manic states.

- Experts refer to sex addiction as a progressive intimacy disorder, which means that it worsens over time.

- According to a leading California treatment center, **42 percent** of sex addicts earn more than **$30,000 a year**, and **58 percent** are college graduates.

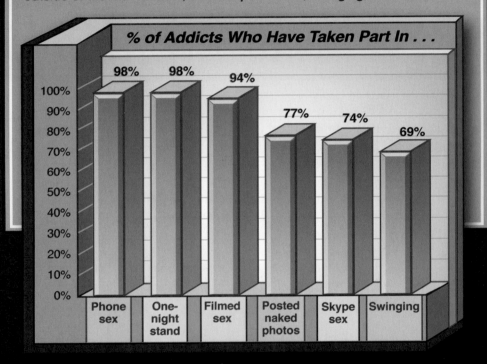

The Sexual Activities of Sex Addicts

According to a survey on sex addictions in the United Kingdom, most sex addicts have taken part in sexual activities that are considered to be outside of the mainstream, such as phone sex, swinging, and filmed sex.

% of Addicts Who Have Taken Part In . . .

	%
Phone sex	98%
One-night stand	98%
Filmed sex	94%
Posted naked photos	77%
Skype sex	74%
Swinging	69%

Source: "Sex Addictions in the U.K.," Addiction Helper Sex Addiction Survey 2013 Infographic, 2013. www.addictionhelper.com.

- According to one national survey, **65 percent** of sex addicts are professionals with a college degree.

- A survey of sex addicts by psychotherapist Paula Hall found that **40 percent** began to have problems with sexual addiction when they were under **16 years old**, and nearly **10 percent** when they were under **10 years old**.

Sex Addicts Usually Have Other Addictions

Researchers have found that 83 percent of sex addicts have other addictions. Drug addiction is the most common coexisting addiction, while compulsive gambling is the least common.

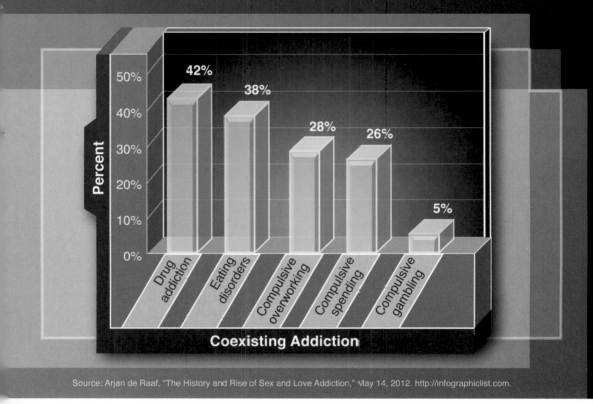

Source: Arjan de Raaf, "The History and Rise of Sex and Love Addiction," May 14, 2012. http://infographiclist.com.

- According to psychiatrist Michael Herkov, about **70 percent** of people who have been convicted of child molestation meet the criteria for sex addiction.

- A study published in *Sexual Addiction & Compulsivity* found that, of **893 heterosexual males** who suffered from a sexual disorder such as sex addiction, **69 percent** had coexisting addictions, including alcoholism, substance abuse, and caffeine addiction.

The Cycle of Sex Addiction

Researchers have identified six steps in the cycle of sex addiction. These steps parallel the steps identified in other behavioral and substance addictions, including alcohol addiction.

Source: Robert Weiss, *Cruise Control*, Kindle edition. Carefree, AZ: Gentle Path, 2013.

- The Sexual Recovery Institute reports that **54 percent** of men do not consider online affairs to be adultery.

- According to a survey by Patrick Carnes, **38 percent** of sex addicts have been to an emergency room for sex-related injuries.

What Is Pornography Addiction?

> **Children's entire expectation of sex had been defined by what they see in online porn. . . . What's now considered 'normal' by under-18s is an entirely distorted view of intercourse.**
>
> —Martin Daubney, an antipornography activist and host of the documentary *Porn on the Brain*.

> **Last semester, I probably spent more time online than I did sleeping. Often, I would go multiple days staying in my room 'porning,' not going to classes, not going to the cafeteria, and eating granola bars for meals.**
>
> —"Atheistic Porn Addict," a male college student who is concerned about his online pornography addiction.

Seventeen-year-old Nathan Haug became addicted to Internet porn at twelve years of age. "So twelve to . . . fourteen, it was there, uninterrupted," he said on ABC's *Nightline*. "I became almost numb to it. It became such a part of my daily routine."[25] The experience made him feel isolated, depressed, and trapped in a cycle of compulsion he did not understand. He eventually went to his parents for help and broke his addiction, but thousands of other teens do not—and their compulsion to use pornography follows them into their adult years. Some experts believe that in the next decade the medical community will see an epidemic of pornography addiction among young adults. According to Patrick J. Carnes, "Two-thirds of kids in junior high are watching pornography while doing their homework. . . . For people who are still wondering if there is even a disease, we have a tsunami coming."[26]

Even though experts warn that pornography addiction will soon reach epidemic proportions, pornography addiction is still not recognized as a disorder by the *DSM*. As it is with sex addiction, not enough research has been done on the effects of pornography to determine if it is truly addictive. According to Gary Wilson, when researchers try to study the effects of pornography, they are not able to find a group of men who have never used it. "Studies have no control groups," Wilson explains. "This creates a huge blind spot."[27] It also lowers the credibility of pornography research in the medical community. Even so, enough is known about other behavioral addictions for experts to be very concerned about the effects of pornography.

> **As it is with sex addiction, not enough research has been done on the effects of pornography to determine if it is truly addictive.**

What Causes Pornography Addiction?

While pornography has been around for centuries, pornography addiction only began to receive widespread attention in the 1990s, when pornographic videos became easily accessible on the Internet. Before that time acquiring porn was expensive, inconvenient, and risky to one's reputation. But once porn moved online, the Internet created what psychologist Jesse Bering calls "the perfect storm for ravenous consumption."[28] Pornography is now affordable (in fact, it is usually free), it can be accessed at any time on any number of mobile devices, and people can view it anonymously with little risk to their reputations. Scholars call this the "Triple A Engine" effect (affordable, accessible, and anonymous). Many clinicians blame this Triple A Engine for the huge increase in patients who are seeking them out for help with pornography addiction.

The experts who believe pornography is addictive compare it to drugs and alcohol. The antiporn organization Fight The New Drug says on its website that "pornography tricks your brain into releasing the same pleasure chemicals that drugs do." This flood of chemicals—which is reinforced by the pleasure of orgasm if an individual is masturbating—is what causes the addiction. When porn releases a surge of dopamine, the brain does two things. First, it creates "new brain pathways that essentially lead the user back to the behavior." Second, it tries "to protect itself from the overload of dopamine by getting rid of some of its chemical receptors."[29] Once this happens, the brain cannot experience pleasure as easily and needs more extreme forms of porn to become aroused. This process of tolerance and escalation, the organization says, is what causes the addiction. As psychiatrist Jeffrey Satinover explained to a US Senate committee, "It is as though we have devised a form of heroin . . . usable in the privacy of one's own home and injected directly to the brain through the eyes."[30]

An Evolutionary Response

While there is no scientific proof that pornography is addictive, there are studies that help explain why it can cause compulsive behavior. Scientists have found that in animals, if a male is allowed to mate with a female as much as he wants, the amount of time it takes him to get aroused again after orgasm gets progressively longer and longer. But if he is given a different female after each orgasm, he gets aroused right away. This evolutionary response assures that males spread their genes to as many females as possible.

> Some Internet porn users prefer to masturbate to pornography than to have intercourse with their partners.

When scientists tested human males to see if this worked with pornography, they found that it did. An Australian study found that men who watched the same erotic scene eighteen times in a row were less and less aroused on each viewing. But when they were showed a different scene the nineteenth time, their arousal increased dramatically. While this might seem like common sense, it explains why some Internet porn users prefer to masturbate to pornography than to have intercourse with their partners. "Internet pornography offers endless fireworks at the click of a mouse," Wilson says. "You can hunt (another dopamine-releasing activity) for hours, and experience more novel sex partners every ten minutes than your hunter-gatherer ancestors experienced in a lifetime."[31]

Escalation and Gonzo Porn

The most popular and lucrative genre of Internet pornography is known as "gonzo" porn. As Gail Dines, author of *Pornland*, explains, gonzo "depicts hard-core, body-punishing sex in which women are demeaned and debased."[32] One reason gonzo porn is so popular is that it rarely includes a plot or story line—which means that viewers do not have to search through a video to get to the sex scenes. Instead they can click from scene to scene, satisfying their craving for variety.

Another reason gonzo porn is popular is because it is designed to shock viewers with depictions of violence or the breaking of cultural taboos. Experts say that viewers like this kind of porn not because they are more sexually deviant than in the past but because they have built up a chemical tolerance to the vast amounts of dopamine released in their brains. Therefore, they need progressively more shocking images and scenarios to become aroused. According to Fight The New Drug, "Many porn users find themselves getting aroused by things that used to disgust them or that go against what they think is morally right."[33] The makers of gonzo porn understand this. They know that once a porn user is addicted, he or she will pay a premium for videos that are progressively more shocking and taboo. According to Dines, the success of pornographers "depends on finding some new, edgy sex act that will draw in users always on the lookout for that extra bit of sexual charge."[34]

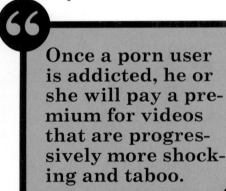

Once a porn user is addicted, he or she will pay a premium for videos that are progressively more shocking and taboo.

Unfortunately, the escalation process sometimes leads pornography addicts to child pornography. Many seek out these images not because they are aroused by children but because they are aroused by the shame and taboo that surrounds child porn. Addicts who have been caught up in the escalation process have been arrested, jailed, and branded sexual predators for life because child pornography has been found on their computers.

How Prevalent Is Pornography Addiction?

How many people are addicted to online pornography is unknown, but there is no doubt about its popularity. According to the website CovenentEyes.com, in the first eight months of 2014 there were over 1.3 billion online searches for pornography. A 2013 AskMen.com survey found that 91 percent of respondents said they watch pornography. Other surveys have found that 68 percent of young adult men and 18 percent of women use porn at least once a week. And a 2012 survey by Tru Research found that 32 percent of teens admit to intentionally accessing online porn.

Most experts believe that teenagers are more vulnerable to pornography addiction than adults. "The way that [teenagers'] brains are set up, they are particularly vulnerable to drugs, to alcohol, to gambling and other behavioral addictions,"[35] explains psychologist Matt Field. One reason is that the impulse control center of the teenaged brain, located in the frontal lobe, is not fully developed. Another reason is that teens have a heightened sensitivity to rewards. Finally, because of hormonal changes, teens also have a heightened sexual response. For all of these reasons, when presented with intense and exciting media like pornography, making smart choices is especially hard for teens to do.

> " When presented with intense and exciting media like pornography, making smart choices is especially hard for teens to do. "

Why Is Pornography Addiction a Problem?

Some experts believe that pornography is a gateway drug to sex addiction. A 2012 study published in *Computers in Human Behavior* found a correlation between pornography use and risky sexual behavior and concluded that "consumption of pornographic media may increase males' probability of engaging in risky sexual behavior by . . . [encouraging] activities such as group sex, paid sex, and extramarital sex."[36] These sexual activities are linked with an increased risk of acquiring sexually transmitted diseases. It is important to note, however, that the study does not prove that pornography use caused or led to risky sexual behavior. It only found a correlation, which means that individuals who use pornography also tend to have risky sex.

Other experts note a high incidence of depression among Internet pornography addicts. Studies have shown a relationship between frequent porn use and feelings of loneliness and despair, and that twice as many people who use Internet porn have severe clinical depression than do non-users. Some users say that the shame they feel over their porn use causes them to withdraw from others. Says former porn addict Breanne Saldivar, in high school "I started to isolate myself because I hated what I was doing. I hated that I couldn't stop."[37]

Harm to Relationships

Pornography addiction harms relationships in several ways. Addicts can withdraw for hours each day to view pornography, neglecting their partners. Spouses who discover their habits often feel as though they have been cheated on, and many choose to end the relationship. The American Academy of Matrimonial Lawyers reported that 56 percent of divorce cases involve issues relating to the compulsive use of Internet pornography.

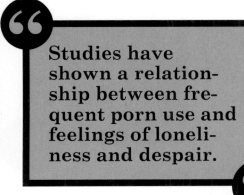

Studies have shown a relationship between frequent porn use and feelings of loneliness and despair.

Some addicts come to enjoy masturbating to pornography more than face-to-face sexual encounters with their partners. As sex therapist Janie Lacy explains, "Porn creates an environment in which everyone is beautiful or handsome. Body parts are perfect, accentuated, and responsive in extreme satisfaction. How can anyone's spouse or partner compete with that?"[38] Porn addicts also become desensitized to dopamine, and the smaller hits released by traditional sex are no longer stimulating. As one porn addict explains, "[Sex is] not as good as masturbating. . . . I'm not getting the pleasure I should be from real girls."[39]

Porn-Induced Erectile Dysfunction (PIED)

The arousal patterns of many male porn addicts have been so habituated to pornography that some of them claim that they are unable to become physically aroused by anything but extremely graphic pornographic images. Others complain that they have lost sensitivity in their genitals and cannot climax without intensely stimulating masturbation.

Most doctors do not consider this type of erectile dysfunction to be a physical problem, and some claim that PIED does not exist. However, more than one hundred thousand people—most of them young men—have joined NoFap to treat PIED and "reboot" their sexual responses. Sixty percent of them have said that after abstaining from masturbation for a period of time, their ability to get physically aroused improved.

Hijacked Sexuality

One of the most destructive effects of pornography addiction is its ability to hijack a person's sexual responses. Many psychologists believe that adults develop their concept of what is arousing on the basis of their most powerful erotic experiences—which normally happen in puberty. In other words, people often fantasize about what turned them on as teenagers. However, pornographic images are so powerful that they can take control of a young person's sexual responses, and a permanent association is made between particular pornographic images and achieving orgasm. According to Dines, "Porn is actually being encoded into a boy's sexual identity."[40]

Isaac Abel has experienced this firsthand. From the age of thirteen until his senior year in high school, he masturbated compulsively to online pornography. When he started having sex with girls he was horrified to find that he could not get an erection without fantasizing about porn. This problem continued into adulthood. "It was a dissociative, alienating, almost inhuman task to close my eyes while having sex with someone I really cared about and . . . recall a deviant video from the archives of my youth that I was ashamed of even then."[41]

Abel is now trying to reprogram himself so that he has some choice over what he thinks about when he has sex. "I can get off without thinking about anything 'shameful' or pornographic," he says, "but it's not as much fun—it physically doesn't feel as good."[42]

People who find themselves in Abel's predicament wish they had known about the effects of pornography when they were younger. However, because the subject can be uncomfortable, many parents do not discuss the potential effects of pornography with their children. In an age when pornography is so readily available, most experts believe that early education is the key to minimizing its effect on today's youth.

What Is Pornography Addiction?

66 **As men have increased ability to view Internet erotica, sex crimes go down. Believe it or not—porn is good for society.** 99

—David J. Ley, *The Myth of Sex Addiction*, Kindle edition. Lanham, MD: Rowman & Littlefield, 2012.

Ley is a clinical psychologist in Albuquerque, New Mexico.

....

66 **Ten years ago there were very few cases where Internet porn was involved in a young person's offending behavior. Now it's the majority.** 99

—John Woods, *Porn on the Brain*, Channel 4 (UK television network), September 30, 2013. www.youtube.com.

Woods is a child and adolescent psychotherapist at the Portman Clinic.

....

Bracketed quotes indicate conflicting positions.

* Editor's Note: While the definition of a primary source can be narrowly or broadly defined, for the purposes of Compact Research, a primary source consists of: 1) results of original research presented by an organization or researcher; 2) eyewitness accounts of events, personal experience, or work experience; 3) first-person editorials offering pundits' opinions; 4) government officials presenting political plans and/or policies; 5) representatives of organizations presenting testimony or policy.

Primary Source Quotes

66 **Porn sets up couples and families to fail because as one becomes more immersed in the false 'reality,' true reality suffers and is shamed.** 99

—Janie Lacy, "Five Reasons Porn Can Hurt Your Love Life," GoodTherapy.org, January 9, 2013. www.goodtherapy.org.

Lacy is a sex therapist and licensed mental health counselor in Maitland, Florida.

66 **The addiction model doesn't necessarily recognize that a little porn here and there may be good for you sometimes.** 99

—Moushumi Ghose, "The Good and Bad Sides of Porn," GoodTherapy.org, June 22, 2011. www.goodtherapy.org.

Ghose is a sex therapist in Los Angeles, California.

66 **Porn creates the unrealistic illusion that your partner should always be ready, willing, and able.** 99

—Janie Lacy, "Five Reasons Porn Can Hurt Your Love Life," GoodTherapy.org, January 9, 2013. www.goodtherapy.org.

Lacy is a sex therapist and licensed mental health counselor in Maitland, Florida.

66 **Watching Internet sexual images can encourage young people to view others as mere sexual objects.** 99

—Jill Denton, "Online Pornography and Youth," GoodTherapy.org, November 7, 2011. www.goodtherapy.org.

Denton is a marriage and family therapist in Los Osos, California.

66 **Neuroscience research has shown that when men watch pornography, the thing they attend to most is a woman's face, not her genitals.** 99

—David J. Ley, *The Myth of Sex Addiction*, Kindle edition. Lanham, MD: Rowman & Littlefield, 2012.

Ley is a clinical psychologist in Albuquerque, New Mexico.

66 If porn does have the insidious power to be addictive, then letting our children consume it freely via the Internet is like leaving heroin lying around the house. **99**

—Martin Daubney, "Experiment That Convinced Me Online Porn Is the Most Pernicious Threat Facing Children Today," MailOnline.com, September 25, 2013. www.dailymail.co.uk.

Daubney is an antipornography activist and host of the documentary *Porn on the Brain*.

66 If [porn is] the only influence kids are getting then they're going to get a very skewed version of what sex is. **99**

—Johnny Hunt, *Porn on the Brain*, Channel 4 (UK television network), September 30, 2013. www.youtube.com.

Hunt is a sex educator and consultant.

66 Young boys are getting their sexual cues from men who are acting like psychopaths. **99**

—Gail Dines, *Porn on the Brain*, Channel 4 (UK television network), September 30, 2013. www.youtube.com.

Dines is a sex educator and author of *Pornland: How Porn Has Hijacked Our Sexuality*.

Facts and Illustrations

What Is Pornography Addiction?

- Sex researchers Ogi Ogas and Sai Gaddam found that **4 percent** of the top million most popular websites are pornographic.

- Ogas and Gaddam found that about **13 percent** of web searches are for erotic content.

- YouPorn, the second largest porn site in the world, logs **100 million** views each day. During its peak hours, **4,000 videos** are accessed per second.

- According to a survey of NoFap, a social media community on Reddit, about **42 percent** of male college students regularly visit pornographic websites, and **12 percent** spend **5 or more hours** a week on online porn.

- According to the Internet filtering software company CovenantEyes, **1 in 5 mobile searches** are for pornography, and almost a quarter of smartphone owners say they have pornographic material on their phones.

- According to the sex education website Respect Yourself, **53 percent** of **10-year-olds** have accessed some kind of pornography on the Internet.

- According to a 2012 survey by Tru Research, **32 percent** of teens admit to accessing online pornography. Of these, **43 percent** do so on a weekly basis.

The Male Sex Drive Is Novelty Seeking

Research done on rats has shown that male rats can climax much more quickly if exposed to a succession of new mates than to only the same mate. This phenomenon, known as the Coolidge Effect, has also been observed in humans who watch pornography. Internet pornography offers unlimited variety, keeping male arousal levels high.

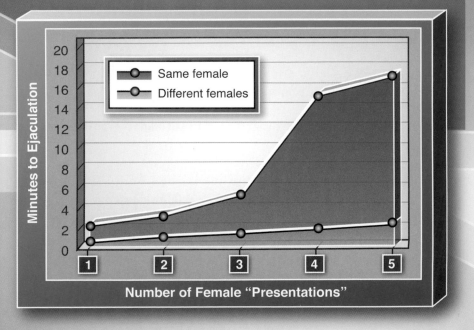

Source: Gary Wilson, "Porn, Novelty, and the Coolidge Effect," Your Brain on Porn, August 8, 2011. www.yourbrainonporn.com.

- According to a 2014 report of online activity by CovenantEyes, **15 percent** of boys and **9 percent** of girls have seen child pornography, **32 percent** of boys and **18 percent** of girls have seen bestiality, and **39 percent** of boys and **18 percent** of girls have seen sexual bondage.

- A 2012 survey of **800 college students** who were regular porn users found that **20 percent** preferred pornography to being sexually intimate with a partner.

Women More Concerned About Partners' Porn Use than Men

In a study of committed heterosexual couples, researchers found that men had significantly lower concerns about their partner's porn use than were women. The study reveals that even casual Internet porn use can have an adverse effect on relationships.

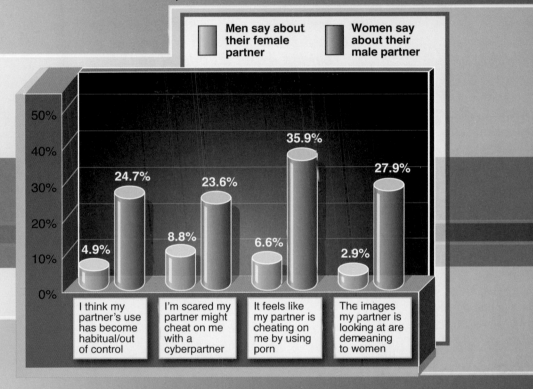

Source: Christian Grov et al., "Perceived Consequences of Casual Online Sexual Activities on Heterosexual Relationships: A U.S. Online Survey," *Archives of Sexual Behavior*, vol. 40, no. 2, April 2011, p. 434.

- According to a study published in the journal *Violence Against Women*, an analysis of over **300 sex scenes** in the most popular online pornographic videos revealed that **88.2 percent** contained physical aggression and **48.7 percent** contained verbal aggression. **Ninety percent** of all scenes contained at least **1 aggressive act**, with an average of nearly **12 acts** of aggression per scene.

Women Believe Porn Interferes with Sex

A 2014 survey of *Essence* magazine readers (who are mostly women) found that the majority believed that pornography changed their expectations about sex. The poll shows that, among the sample of respondents, pornography may be interfering with their satisfaction with sex.

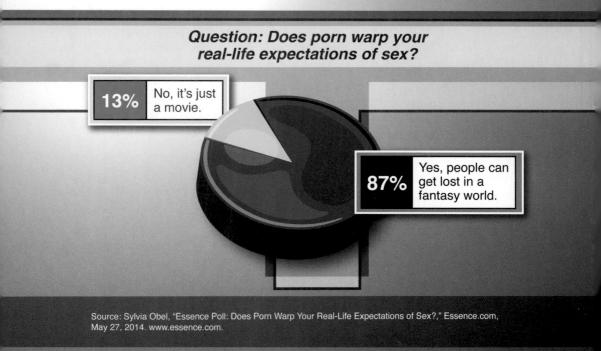

Question: Does porn warp your real-life expectations of sex?

13% No, it's just a movie.

87% Yes, people can get lost in a fantasy world.

Source: Sylvia Obel, "Essence Poll: Does Porn Warp Your Real-Life Expectations of Sex?," Essence.com, May 27, 2014. www.essence.com.

- According to a study published in *Social Science Quarterly*, Internet users who have had an extramarital affair were **3.18 times more likely** to have used online pornography than those who had remained faithful to their partners.

- A study published in *Sexual Addiction & Compulsivity* found that among the **68 percent** of couples in which one person was addicted to Internet porn, one or both had lost interest in sex.

Can Sex and Pornography Addictions Be Overcome?

66Like other types of addicts, some sexual addicts may never be 'cured.' Sexual addicts achieve a state of recovery, but maintaining that recovery can be a lifelong, day-by-day process.**99**

— International Institute for Trauma and Addiction Professionals, which trains and certifies sexual addiction professionals.

66When sex addicts complete their treatment, they're still addicts, facing a lifetime of recovery. When someone completes sex therapy, psychotherapy, or couples counseling—really completes it—they've changed.**99**

— Marty Klein, a sex therapist and international lecturer on sexuality and public policy.

In the 2013 film *Thanks for Sharing* recovering sex addict Dede finds herself outside of her ex-boyfriend's apartment. She frantically calls Neil, a new friend from her 12-step sex addiction recovery group. Neil, who also was on the verge of acting out sexually, hurries to her aid, and the two help each other. Robert Weiss notes that this is an "excellent depiction of the need for social support in recovery. Addicts do not get sober or stay sober in isolation."[43]

Twelve-step programs are just one of the many treatment options for sex and pornography addicts. More and more therapists are specializing in sex addiction, and rehabilitation centers for substance abuse are expanding their programs to include sex addiction treatment. Christian sex-addiction recovery groups are popping up all over the country. And the Internet—which enables many facets of sex addiction—is also a place where addicts can reach out to each other for support. In fact, NoFap recently passed the one-hundred-thousand-member mark.

12-Step Programs

Sex Addicts Anonymous (SAA) was the first of four 12-step programs in the United States that dealt exclusively with sex addiction. (The other three are Sexaholics Anonymous, Sex and Love Addicts Anonymous, and Sexual Compulsives Anonymous.) SAA was formed by a group of men in Minnesota in the 1970s—long before the term *sex addiction* became commonplace. Twelve-step programs such as SAA adapt the format used in Alcoholics Anonymous, modifying the twelve steps of recovery to fit the addiction being addressed. Members meet, share their struggles, and offer each other support and guidance. According to *Time*, 5 million to 10 million people in the United States attend one of these four 12-step programs. SAA has about twelve hundred meetings worldwide, and it estimates that from between 2004 and 2011 it grew about 10 percent a year.

> "Twelve-step programs . . . are the best way to help addicts deal with the often crippling level of shame they feel about their behavior.

Experts claim that the 12-step or group therapy format is very effective in treating sex addiction—especially if it is used in conjunction with other forms of therapy. According to the American Association for Marriage and Family Therapy, "Group work is strongly recommended because it affords the recovering addict both support and accountability. Within 12-step groups, it is common to seek out a sponsor with whom one can work through the 12-steps and check-in regarding sobriety."[44] Twelve-step programs not only offer the benefit of accountability to others, but they also are the best way to help addicts deal with the often crippling level of shame they feel about their behavior. Just knowing that others struggle with the same issues can be extremely therapeutic.

Sexual Sobriety

Like Alcoholics Anonymous, sexual addiction 12-step groups use the concept of sobriety. However, most only expect abstinence from sexual activity for the first thirty days, and some programs do not limit sex with a primary partner at all. After the abstinence period, the addict comes up with a sexual sobriety plan. Sexaholics Anonymous defines sexual sobriety as sex within marriage, and claims that "for the sexaholic, any form of sex with one's self or with partners other than the spouse is progressively addictive and destructive."[45]

Other recovery groups define sobriety as refraining from all sexual activity that does not support healthy connectedness to another human being. But usually addicts define for themselves what sobriety is by examining their personal values and listing specific sexual activities that are in line with their values or are not. At the Sexual Recovery Institute, Weiss has his patients create and sign a behavioral contract that spells out what behavior is allowable and what is not. "We treat it very much like sobriety for an eating disorder," he says. "They have to define for themselves based on their own goals and belief systems: 'What is healthy eating for me? Can I go to a buffet? Can I eat by myself?' We look at your goals and figure in your sexual behaviors and validate what's going to lead you back to the behavior you don't want to do."[46]

Triggering Behavior

An important part of sexual sobriety is defining and eliminating situations and behaviors that can trigger sexual acting out, pushing addicts into the cycle of addiction. Every addict's triggers are different. In *Thanks for Sharing*, one addict had the television removed from his hotel room whenever he traveled for business so he would not be tempted to watch pornography. Another, who was addicted to frottage (obtaining sexual stimulation by rubbing against a person or object), never took the subway because the temptation to act out was too great. Other addicts avoid places where they may encounter scantily clad people, like the beach. Some even avoid handling dollar bills because it reminds them of tipping at strip clubs.

Researchers have found that once the origin of a person's addiction is uncovered, it is easier to predict what might be a trigger. People with trauma-related sex addiction, such as those who were physically or emotionally abused as children, are often triggered by anxiety. Those with attachment-related addiction, such as those who failed to bond with their caretakers as children, are often triggered by feelings of loneliness and insecurity. And those with opportunity-related addiction, which includes the majority of pornography addicts, can be triggered by feelings of entitlement.

Christian Recovery

The Christian Recovery movement seeks to help people overcome their addictions through faith and religious teachings. There is an element of religion in Alcoholics Anonymous, which holds many of its meetings in church basements and requires that addicts turn their lives over to a "higher power." The Christian Recovery movement takes this a step further, relying on Christian values to define what types of sexual contact are acceptable and what types are not.

> "The Christian Recovery move-ment . . . [relies] on Christian values to define what types of sexual contact is acceptable and what types are not.

Recovery takes many forms. Some organizations form step-based recovery groups of their own, including L.I.F.E. Recovery International, which organizes recovery groups and offers guidance in the form of a prescribed month-by-month program. Other organizations hold seminars, such as the New Life Ministries of Laguna Beach, California, which runs a three-day seminar for men. And some conduct recovery entirely online, such as XXXChurch.com. The website focuses on pornography addiction, allows addicts to share or confess online, and holds local events. XXXChurch also sells a type of Internet filtering software known as accountability software, which blocks pornographic sites or informs a designated "accountability partner" if pornographic sites are accessed.

Recovery Online

Because pornography addiction is largely a problem that plays out on the Internet, many pornography-related recovery programs are online. One of the largest is NoFap. Although not everyone who is a member identifies as a pornography addict, most believe that excessive masturbation is lowering their sex drive or causing erectile dysfunction. Other online support groups encourage addicts to pledge to abstain from using online porn and to spread the word about the dangers of pornography addiction.

Inpatient Treatment Centers

The news is full of reports of celebrities such as actor David Duchovny, professional golfer Tiger Woods, and comedian Russell Brand checking into rehab centers for sex addiction. Most of these are drug and alcohol inpatient treatment centers that have added a sex addiction program. A few have robust programs dedicated solely to sex addiction, such as the Sexual Recovery Institute, which also offers treatment for pornography addiction and love addiction, and has specific programs for gay men, couples, and nonviolent offenders.

Sex rehab programs usually last for three to six weeks, though some intensive programs are shorter, and longer stays are usually an option. Patients spend the first portion of their stay acclimating to abstaining from sex and masturbation. Since the Internet usually is a component in both sex and pornography addiction, there are usually no opportunities for patients to get online. Personal relationships with the opposite sex are carefully monitored, and flirting is discouraged. Some centers keep patients under video surveillance. According to psychiatrist Charles Sophy, patients are encouraged

> "[Patients] work with counselors to try to discover the root cause of their addiction and create a sobriety plan to deal with future temptation.

to concentrate on their own recovery, and the restrictions are about "removing outside noise so that patients can hear the noise coming from within and try to understand it."[47] After a period of adjustment, patients move onto individual and group therapy. They work with counselors to try to discover the root cause of their addiction and create a sobriety plan to deal with future temptation. Most rehab centers also include the family in counseling. All encourage individuals to continue their recovery after they leave the center by joining 12-step programs and seeking therapy.

Outpatient Therapy

Because sex addiction is not an official diagnosis, many psychologists, therapists, and even addiction specialists do not know much about it. Addicts seeking help should make sure that their therapist is knowledgeable about sex addiction. The International Institute for Trauma and Addiction Professionals (IITAP), founded by Patrick J. Carnes, offers a Certified Sex Addiction Therapist (CSAT) certification, which indicates that a therapist has had special training in sex addiction. Many qualified therapists do not have a CSAT certification, however, and the certification is not required to treat sex addiction.

Many types of therapists specialize in sex addiction, including marriage and relationship therapists and addiction counselors. However, because sex addicts often have coexisting mental health issues and a history of childhood trauma, traditional therapy with a psychologist or a licensed clinical social worker who specializes in sexual compulsions is usually recommended. These professionals have extensive knowledge about the relationship between mental health and behavioral health, and many work with psychiatrists who can prescribe appropriate medication as needed. Psychiatrists can also prescribe medication that has the side effect of lowering sex drive.

Cognitive Behavioral Therapy (CBT) is an effective treatment style for combating behavioral problems, including behavioral addictions. CBT teaches patients to carefully examine their own thinking process, identify problematic patterns, and come up with ways to short-circuit the process. People undergoing CBT often keep detailed journals of their thought processes. Therapy usually does not dwell on processing childhood issues; instead, it focuses on current circumstances and behaviors. Not all therapists practice CBT as it is a rigorous process that requires special training.

Educating Young People

Pornography addiction has become a particular concern for young people, who find online pornography as preteens and quickly become addicted. Many efforts to combat pornography addiction focus on educating young people before addiction takes hold. One such program is Fight The New Drug (FTND), a web-based advocacy and education group.

FTND asks kids to take an online pledge not to use pornography and to help spread the word about its dangers. It also has an online video recovery program that is free to anyone under twenty-one years old. FTND speaks at schools and community centers around the country.

Other antipornography advocates believe that most young people seek out pornography online because they are curious about sex. "[Kids] want to know how you have sex, what you do, where it goes, how to be good at it, and what it should look like,"[48] explains Johnny Hunt, a sex education consultant who talks to middle school students in explicit terms about sex. Hunt starts out by asking students to list all of the sex-related words that they know, and he is often surprised by the terms they have picked up from watching pornography. Gail Dines is not. "When [a thirteen-year-old boy] puts 'porn' into Google . . . he is catapulted into a world of sexual violence, sexual cruelty, [and] body punishing sex,"[49] she writes in *Pornland*. Pornography is giving many young kids a skewed perception of what sex is, and some do not recognize that what they see on the Internet is very different from how they should be behaving.

> " Pornography is giving many young kids a skewed perception of what sex is. "

Educators like Hunt and Amy Danahay, who manages the website Respect Yourself, hope to change that. "The Internet has changed how young people find out about sex," she says. "It would be naïve to think that many young people are not regularly accessing far more explicit material and if we want to give them access to relevant information, we have to move with the times."[50] Respect Yourself offers explicit—and sometimes graphic—information about sex and stresses that pornographic movies do not reflect reality. According to the site, "Porn is entertainment designed to excite you. . . . You don't believe that everything you see in the cinema is real. . . . Porn is no different."[51]

Primary Source Quotes*

Can Sex and Pornography Addictions Be Overcome?

66 **The admission of powerlessness over one's addiction is the first defeat of infantile egoism—a first step in the assumption of responsibility.** 99

—Dorothy Hayden, "How the 12 Steps Heal Sex Addicts: Step One," It's Cheating: Infidelity in the Digital Age, August 17, 2011. www.itscheating.com.

Hayden is a sex addiction expert and licensed clinical social worker in New York City.

66 **This belief, that one's sexuality is an uncontrollable force, can become a self-fulfilling prophecy.** 99

—David J. Ley, *The Myth of Sex Addiction*, Kindle edition. Lanham, MD: Rowman & Littlefield, 2012.

Ley is a clinical psychologist in Albuquerque, New Mexico.

Bracketed quotes indicate conflicting positions.

* Editor's Note: While the definition of a primary source can be narrowly or broadly defined, for the purposes of Compact Research, a primary source consists of: 1) results of original research presented by an organization or researcher; 2) eyewitness accounts of events, personal experience, or work experience; 3) first-person editorials offering pundits' opinions; 4) government officials presenting political plans and/or policies; 5) representatives of organizations presenting testimony or policy.

66 There are now several quite good filtering and accountability software programs that sex addicts can install on their digital equipment. These programs are an excellent way for sex addicts to protect themselves from themselves. 99

—Robert Weiss, "Filtering and Accountability Softwares for Use in Sex Addiction Recovery," Robert Weiss MSW, 2014. www.robertweissmsw.com.

Weiss is a sex addiction expert and founder of the Sexual Recovery Institute.

66 There simply is no perfect [Internet] filter. 99

—Barry Collins, *Porn on the Brain*, Channel 4 (UK television network), September 30, 2013. www.youtube.com.

Collins is the editor of *PC Pro* magazine, which completed a study on the latest Internet filtering software.

66 For most [sex addicts], a period of celibacy and abstinence from masturbation can be useful to allow old neural pathways to begin to die. 99

—Paula Hall, *Understanding and Treating Sex Addiction*, Kindle edition. New York: Routledge, 2013.

Hall is a sex addiction therapist and founder of The Hall Recovery Course.

66 [Sex addiction treatment] programs aim far too low—to create life-long recovery rather than resolution and permanent change—and focus way too much on sex. 99

—Marty Klein, "If It Isn't Sex Addiction, How Do You Treat It? (Part 2)," *Sexual Intelligence* (blog), November 1, 2013.

Klein is a sex therapist and international lecturer on sexuality and public policy.

"Fifteen years ago, my average patient was probably 40 to 50 years old. Now, University students—18, 19, 20—are very routine."

—Jon E. Grant, *Porn on the Brain*, Channel 4 (UK television network), September 30, 2013. www.youtube.com.

Grant is a neuroscientist at the University of Chicago.

"We need to be talking about these things [sex] so that when children start accessing porn, it comes up as everyday conversation."

—Amy Danahay, *Porn on the Brain*, Channel 4 (UK television network), September 30, 2013. www.youtube.com.

Danahay is the project manager for the sex education website Respect Yourself.

Facts and Illustrations

Can Sex and Pornography Addictions Be Overcome?

- A Sex Addiction Therapist certification requires **120 hours** of classroom work and **30 hours** of clinical supervision.

- Evidence suggests that attending a **12-step** support group while in treatment for sex addiction can significantly aid recovery.

- According to Patrick Carnes, about **17 percent** of sex addicts who seek professional treatment have attempted suicide, and **72 percent** have thought about suicide obsessively.

- In a survey of about **1,000 female sex addicts**, **40 percent** have experienced unwanted pregnancies, and **36 percent** have had at least **1 abortion**.

- Residential sex addiction treatment centers can cost **$37,000** a month and up.

- **Thirty-one percent** of the people who have joined NoFap, the online support group for compulsive masturbators, are teenagers aged **13 to 19**.

- A NoFap survey found that about **60 percent** of people who quit masturbating felt that their sexual dysfunctions had improved.

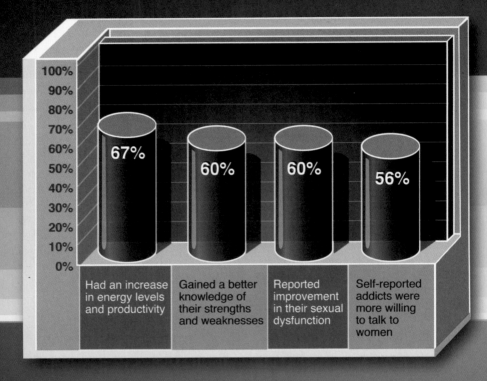

Benefits of Abstaining from Pornography and Masturbation

Members of the self-help group NoFap (*fap* is a slang term for masturbation) found that abstaining from pornography and masturbation had significant benefits. Over half saw improvements in physical problems like erectile dysfunction. Most also had improvements in energy, personal insight, and even in their willingness to flirt.

Had an increase in energy levels and productivity	Gained a better knowledge of their strengths and weaknesses	Reported improvement in their sexual dysfunction	Self-reported addicts were more willing to talk to women
67%	60%	60%	56%

Source: "Taking a Whack Out of Porn," Infographic, ProjectKnow.com, 2013.

- An analysis of **46 studies** on the effects of pornography concluded that viewing pornographic material increases an individual's risk of committing sexual offenses by **22 percent**.

- According to psychologist David J. Ley, **100 percent** of the people who seek sex addiction treatment have a mental illness, a personality disorder, or a second addiction.

Identifying Triggers

Experts believe that childhood trauma and abuse, attachment disorders, and exposure to excessive amounts of pornography can lead to sex addiction. Researchers have found that each of these root causes has a different set of triggers—feelings or situations that can cause an addict to act out. Sex addiction therapists help addicts identify and avoid these triggers to prevent relapse. In the accompanying table, common triggers are listed for each cause.

Childhood Trauma–Related Sex Addiction	Attachment-Related Sex Addiction	Opportunity-Related Sex Addiction (Pornography Addiction)
When life is particularly stressful	Arguing with a loved one	Empty house
When life feels out of control	Feeling overwhelmed by responsibility	Unprotected Internet
When life feels empty and meaningless	Feeling trapped by another's need	Being away from home
Feeling fearful	Feeling unable to confront a loved one	Feeling stressed
Feeling powerless	Feeling rejected	Feeling sorry for yourself
Feeling anxious	Feeling lonely	Feeling entitled
Feeling depressed	Feeling left out	Feeling ashamed
Feeling vulnerable	Feeling undervalued	Being flattered or flirted with
Needing to be strong and fight	Feeling defensive	Being with certain people

Source: Paula Hall, *Understanding and Treating Sex Addiction*, Kindle edition. New York: Routledge, 2013.

Parent-Child Communication and Porn Use

In a survey of fourteen- to sixteen-year-olds in one secondary school in the United Kingdom, over 80 percent said they had viewed online pornography at home. Almost as many also said their parents had never discussed online pornography with them. Some experts say that parents can help their children avoid or overcome pornography addiction by discussing the dangers of online pornography.

14–16-year-olds	
Say that they look at online porn while they are at home:	81%
Say their parents have never discussed online porn with them:	75%

Source: Psychologies, "Put Porn in Its Place," August 2010. https://psychologies.co.uk/put-porn-in-its-place.

- According to Carnes, overcoming sex addiction can take **3 to 5 years**.

- Research has shown that it is important for an addict to overcome feelings of shame in treatment because feeling shame is likely to increase addictive behavior.

- On the day that actor David Duchovny announced he was checking into a sex addiction rehab center, **50,000 people** visited the website sexhelp.com, crashing their servers.

Are Sex and Pornography Really Addictive?

> **66** The narrative of porn as an external factor that takes over your system is a false (and overwhelmingly Christian) explanation that fails to recognize sexual histories and user conceptions of sexuality. **99**
>
> —Jessi Fischer, a sex educator in San Francisco, CA.

> **66** Compulsive pornography users do have parallels with substance use disorders. **99**
>
> —Valerie Voon, a neuropsychiatrist at the University of Cambridge.

66 In thirty-one years as a sex therapist, marriage counselor, and psychotherapist, I've never seen sex addiction,"[52] writes Marty Klein. Klein is one of a growing number of critics who say that the diagnosis of sex or pornography addiction is not "clinically valuable."[53] Another expert calls it a "dangerous fraud."[54] Some claim that there simply is not scientific evidence to support the addiction model. Others point out the harm that the label "sex addict" can do to an individual. While these critics do not doubt that some people are suffering because of their sexual compulsions, they say that calling dysfunctional behavior a disease can do much more harm than good.

Rewiring the Brain

Even though the medical community cannot agree on a single definition of addiction, most do agree that addiction is a brain disease. Addictive substances rewire the reward pathways in the brain, which changes behavior. In other words, addiction is something physical that happens to a person's brain, regardless of his or her mental strength or willpower. According to the National Institute on Drug Abuse:

> When addiction takes over, a person's ability to exert self-control can become seriously impaired. Brain imaging studies from drug-addicted individuals show physical changes in areas of the brain that are critical to judgment, decisionmaking, learning and memory, and behavior control. Scientists believe that these changes alter the way the brain works, and may help explain the compulsive and destructive behaviors of addiction.[55]

Critics of the sexual addiction model say that only drugs are powerful enough to rewire the brain enough to cause addiction. Natural behaviors like eating or having sex release just a fraction of the dopamine—the chemical that tells our brain what it should want—that powerful drugs like heroin and cocaine release. Critics claim there simply is not enough hard data about sexual addiction to support the theory that it rewires the brain. They point out that addiction proponents like Patrick J. Carnes and Robert Weiss base their theories on studies of other substances and behaviors. As Klein states, there is "not a shred of evidence . . . about how people become addicted to their own body chemicals."[56]

> **Critics of the sexual addiction model say that only drugs are powerful enough to rewire the brain.**

That may soon change. A few initial studies have been completed that support the theory that sex and pornography can be addictive. In 2014 neuropsychiatrist Valerie Voon published a study that showed that when sex and pornography addicts looked at pornographic images, the pleasure centers of their brains "lit up" with the same intensity of electrical activity as was observed in drug addicts. A second study in Germany got similar results. Both studies were small, and much more research needs to be done, but initial findings do indicate that sex and pornography affect the brain much more strongly than was previously thought.

Critics like Klein claim that the studies do not prove addiction because addiction is not defined by brain activity. "That's the same part of the brain that lights up when we see a sunset, the Golden Gate Bridge, the perfect donut, a gorgeous touchdown pass, or our grandchild's smile," Klein writes. "Our brain, our blood, and our hormones always react to pleasure—including sexual pleasure."[57]

Is Addiction Something Other than a Brain Disease?

In 2013 the APA admitted one behavioral addiction into the *DSM*: gambling disorder. Critics of the sexual addiction model are concerned that this paves the way for other behavioral addictions to be included in the *DSM*. According to psychiatrist Allen Frances, "*DSM-5* has created a slippery slope by introducing the concept of Behavioral Addictions that eventually can spread to make a mental disorder of everything we like to do a lot."[58]

Because of the controversy over substance versus behavioral addictions, some addiction specialists think the brain disease model of addiction should be abandoned altogether. Stanton Peele believes that the criteria for addiction should be how badly a substance or behavior harms a person's life, not how it impacts the brain. "People aren't addicted unless they experience a range of disruptive problems—no matter how addictive the same drug may be for others,"[59] he explains. Peele believes that it is illogical that gambling addiction is now considered to be a brain disease, yet other behavioral addictions are not. As he writes in *Psychology Today*, "Is gambling really more neurologically, or intensely, rewarding than sex?"[60]

The Problem with Powerlessness

According to most 12-step programs, the first step to sexual sobriety is to admit "we were powerless over addictive sexual behavior—that our lives had become unmanageable."[61] This notion of powerlessness is at the heart of the debate over whether sex and pornography are addictive.

Those who support the addiction model believe that the concept of being powerless over sexual desire reduces the social stigma attached to cheating or being promiscuous and encourages people to seek help. Critics say it encourages people to use the label of sex addiction as an excuse for infidelity. Most people agree with this; polls consistently show that the majority of Americans think that sex addiction is not a disease. As Gwyneth Paltrow's character in *Thanks for Sharing* says to her lover when he admits he is a recovering sex addict, "Isn't that something that guys just say when they get caught cheating?"[62]

> **This notion of powerlessness is at the heart of the debate over whether sex and pornography are addictive.**

According to psychologist David J. Ley, the concept of powerlessness is ultimately harmful to the individual: "Such labeling is counterproductive to helping people take responsibility for their lives, their futures, and their behaviors."[63] Ley notes that many people who pursue traditional therapy for sexual compulsions recover completely, yet a sex addict who attends a 12-step program is labeled an addict for life by the organization. Essentially, 12-step programs claim that sex addicts are forever powerless against their sexual drives and may never resume normal sexual behavior.

Misdiagnosis

Another argument against the addiction model is that it often ignores underlying mental health disorders such as depression and bipolar disorder. In addition, sex addicts are likely to have suffered some form of childhood trauma, and many have a personality disorder. Finally, many sex and pornography addicts have coexisting addictions such as drug and alcohol dependence. None of these mental health issues are caused by sex or pornography, and most should be treated by a skilled psychotherapist—and possibly with medication prescribed by a psychiatrist.

However, according to Klein, while licensed sex therapists are trained to recognize and treat a variety of neuroses and mental disorders, most sex addiction therapists are not—and 12-step programs offer no professional help whatsoever. He states, "Anyone who says 'sexually, I'm out of control' is automatically welcomed into the fellowship of sex addicts—without any attempt to evaluate that person's mental state."[64] Klein argues that sending a person who is making bad sexual choices to a sex addiction clinic is like sending a person with obsessive-compulsive disorder to a hand-washing clinic—the underlying problem is never addressed.

Can Nonmonogamy Be Healthy?

According to sexual addiction specialists, healthy sexual expression can only happen within a committed, emotionally connected, monogamous relationship. For instance, Weiss describes sex addiction as "the obsessive pursuit of non-intimate sexual encounters."[65] And the SAST, the sex addiction screening test created by Patrick J. Carnes, has many questions about nonintimate sex that act as flags for addiction—such as: "Have you maintained multiple romantic or sexual relationships at the same time?"[66]

However, sex addiction critics like Ley claim that there is no one "normal" or "healthy" way to have sex. When one considers the scope of human history, Ley explains, monogamy is not the norm among humans. Even in modern times many Latin American and Asian cultures equate male promiscuity with virility, and European countries such as France and the Netherlands do not see infidelity as a moral failing. According to sex educator and gay activist Dan Savage, "Men were never expected to be monogamous. Men had concubines, mistresses and access to prostitutes, until everybody decided marriage had to be egalitarian and fair"[67] and men had to be as faithful as women. Savage and other critics believe that the diagnosis of sex addiction explains this natural male drive to have multiple partners in a way that is culturally acceptable. According to Ley, women are more likely to stay married to men who are diagnosed with an addiction than to men who choose to be unfaithful.

These critics also point out that consensual nonmonogamy has been

> " Sending a person who is making bad sexual choices to a sex addiction clinic is like sending a person with obsessive-compulsive disorder to a hand-washing clinic. "

gaining popularity in America. Sex researcher Zhana Vrangalova found that about 4 to 5 percent of the US heterosexual population—or 10 million to 20 million people—are engaged in some form of consensual nonmonogamy. And a recent study at the University of Michigan found that even more are interested in exploring it. Furthermore, multiple studies have found that young people—many of them children of divorce—increasingly do not believe in monogamy, marriage, or traditional families. Critics like Savage claim that the problem with the sex addiction model is that it classifies all of these alternatives to monogamy as unhealthy. It does not take into account the variety of human experience and only advocates one model of sexuality.

Alternative Sexuality

The emphasis on sex within monogamous marriage as being the only healthy expression of sex also excludes alternative sexuality. Many of the questions on the SAST have to do with sexual expression that is not in the mainstream, such as "Do you visit sexual bath-houses, sex clubs or video/bookstores as part of your regular sexual activity?" or "Have you regularly engaged in sadomasochistic behavior?"[68] However, Ley points out that as much as 12 percent of the population has engaged in alternative expressions of sexuality at least once. There is also evidence that relationships in the alternative sex community are carefully and rigorously negotiated and are characterized by mutual trust. In fact, a 2013 study published in the *Journal of Sexual Medicine* found that people who practice alternative expressions of sexuality actually scored better on many indicators of mental health than those who did not. According to the author of the study, psychologist Andreas Wismeijer, "We did not have any findings suggesting that people who practice [alternative sexuality] have a damaged psychological profile or have some sort of psychopathology or personality disorder."[69] By categorizing these behaviors as unhealthy or as

> About 4 to 5 percent of the US heterosexual population—or 10 million to 20 million people—are engaged in some form of consensual nonmonogamy.

symptoms of an addiction, critics believe Carnes is further stigmatizing an already marginalized sector of society.

Motivated by Profit

A final criticism of the sexual addictions field is that it is not driven by hard data but by the profit motives of therapists who have found a way to make money from infidelity. Alexandra Katehakis says that demand for sex addiction therapy has been driven by celebrity sex scandals. "Celebrities have been the greatest evangelists for treatment," Katehakis claims. "My practice wouldn't exist without them."[70] According to Katehakis, when public figures claim that sex addiction is the reason for their infidelity, people begin to wonder if they—or their spouses—are also victims.

Critics say that it is this opportunity for profit that is driving the sexual addiction industry. And the industry is extremely profitable. A month's treatment at The Meadows costs over $37,000, and the center takes in almost $2 million a month in revenue. New Life Ministries' three-day seminar costs $1,400, which does not include lodging. Even the nonprofit organization Fight The New Drug charges its "Street Team" members $20 for its Action Kit—a packet of flyers and a tee shirt intended to raise awareness about pornography addiction.

> " When public figures claim that sex addiction is the reason for their infidelity, people begin to wonder if they— or their spouses— are also victims. "

Furthermore, each time a celebrity sex scandal breaks or a new book or movie about sex addiction is released, the media publishes quotes from sex addiction specialists about the dangers of pornography and promiscuous sex. According to Ley, "The professionals who feed the media's need for psychological and biological explanations of sexual behaviors are the same professionals who make very good livings providing treatment services to individuals who self-identify with sexual addiction after hearing these doctors and therapists on television."[71] Certified marriage educator Cathy Meyer claims that this is how the sex addiction industry markets its product—that product being a ready-made excuse for infidelity that conveniently brings people in for treatment. "What better excuse when caught than 'I'm a sex addict?'"[72] she asks.

The debate about whether sex and pornography can cause addiction in the brain is far from over. Regardless of whether these activities are found to cause true addiction, compulsive sexual behavior can destroy relationships and cause individuals emotional pain and suffering. Critics and supporters alike believe that more research into the effects of sex and pornography is needed so that these individuals and families can get the help that they need.

Primary Source Quotes*

Are Sex and Pornography Really Addictive?

66 The field of sex addiction is a belief system, not a scientific or medical school of thought.99

—David J. Ley, *The Myth of Sex Addiction*, Kindle edition. Lanham, MD: Rowman & Littlefield, 2012.

Ley is a clinical psychologist in Albuquerque, New Mexico.

66 Sex addiction is not a moral issue, it is a mental health issue.99

—Paula Hall, *Understanding and Treating Sex Addiction*, Kindle edition. New York: Routledge, 2013.

Hall is a sex addiction therapist and the founder of The Hall Recovery Course.

Bracketed quotes indicate conflicting positions.

* Editor's Note: While the definition of a primary source can be narrowly or broadly defined, for the purposes of Compact Research, a primary source consists of: 1) results of original research presented by an organization or researcher; 2) eyewitness accounts of events, personal experience, or work experience; 3) first-person editorials offering pundits' opinions; 4) government officials presenting political plans and/or policies; 5) representatives of organizations presenting testimony or policy.

Primary Source Quotes

66 The diagnosis of sex addiction is in many ways a diagnosis of discomfort with one's own sexuality, or of being at odds with cultural definitions of normal sex. 99

—Marty Klein, "You're Addicted to What?," *Humanist*, June 28, 2012. http://thehumanist.com.

Klein is a sex therapist and international lecturer on sexuality and public policy.

66 It's hard for us to accept that other people's most intimate desires are different from our own—and when confronted with this fact, we often dismiss their desires as deviant or dangerous or just plain hurtful. 99

—Ogi Ogas and Sai Gaddam, *A Billion Wicked Thoughts: What the World's Largest Experiment Reveals About Human Desire*, Kindle edition. New York: Dutton, 2011.

Ogas and Gaddam received their PhDs in computational neuroscience from Boston University.

66 For the most part, science hasn't kept pace with the cataclysmic shift in pornography's effects on human sexuality. 99

—Jesse Bering, "Dear Jesse, I'm an Atheistic Porn Addict," *Bering in Mind* (blog), *Scientific American*, January 23, 2012. http://blogs.scientificamerican.com.

Bering is a psychologist and author.

66 Watch out for careless over-diagnosis of Internet and sex addiction and the development of lucrative treatment programs to exploit these new markets. 99

—Allen Frances, "*DSM-5* Is a Guide, Not a Bible—Simply Ignore Its 10 Worst Changes," *Psychiatric Times*, December 4, 2012. www.psychiatrictimes.com.

Frances is a psychiatrist, author, and former chair of the *DSM-IV* revision task force.

66 [Endorsing sex addiction] creates a very dangerous slippery slope of moral relativism, where any socially unacceptable behavior is labeled a mental disorder subject to psychiatric treatment.99

—David J. Ley, *The Myth of Sex Addiction*, Kindle edition. Lanham, MD: Rowman & Littlefield, 2012.

Ley is a clinical psychologist in Albuquerque, New Mexico.

66 The addiction model starts with 'We admitted we were powerless.' The therapy model starts with 'You're responsible for your choices; I wonder why you keep doing what gives you what you say you don't want?'99

—Marty Klein, "You're Addicted to What?," *Humanist*, June 28, 2012. http://thehumanist.com.

Klein is a sex therapist and international lecturer on sexuality and public policy.

Are Sex and Pornography Really Addictive?

- According to the American Psychological Association, there is not enough scientific research to support the claim that sex or pornography is addictive.

- Many psychologists are not trained in distinguishing sexual addiction from normal sexual behavior. A 2010 study of psychologists found that less than half receive adequate training in the nature of healthy sexuality or in the range of normal sexual behaviors.

- No published scientific research supports the claim that treatment providers who complete the Certified Sex Addiction Therapist (CSAT) training program are effective at treating sex addiction.

- No scientific evidence supports the claim that sex addicts experience withdrawal in the medical sense, which is a symptom of sex addiction. The commonly reported symptoms of nervousness, feeling on edge, and preoccupation with thoughts of sex do not qualify as clinical withdrawal.

- In opposition to the claim that watching pornography leads to violence against women, US Justice Department statistics show that since 1995, when Internet pornography became popular, the incidence of sexual violence in the United States has dropped by **64 percent**.

Many People Say Sex Addiction Is Not a Medical Condition

When asked whether sex addiction is a medical condition, many of those polled said it was not. A 2014 poll found that 48 percent of people surveyed did not think sex addiction was a medical condition, as compared to 31 percent who thought that it was (the remaining 21 percent did not respond). Of the eleven mental health issues on the poll, participants were the most skeptical about the validity of sex addiction.

Is not a medical condition   Is a medical condition

Schizophrenia
9% — 81%

Depression
15% — 76%

Anxiety disorder
14% — 75%

Chronic fatigue syndrome
8% — 73%

Anorexia
16% — 68%

Dyslexia
18% — 67%

ADHD
19% — 65%

Obsessive-compulsive disorder
27% — 62%

Compulsive overeating disorder
35% — 52%

Alcoholism
46% — 50%

Sex addiction
48% — 31%

Source: Peter Moore, "Depression a 'Medical Condition,' but Many Wouldn't Seek Help," YouGov, June 19, 2014. https://today.yougov.com.

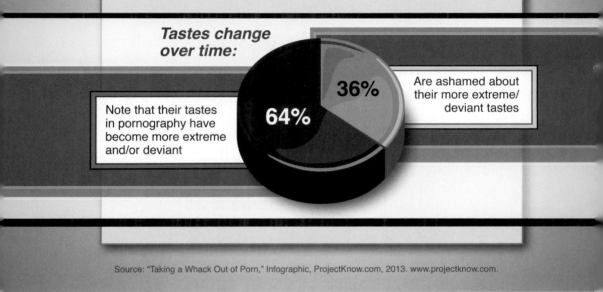

Over Time, Tastes in Porn Become More Extreme

In a 2012 survey of over fifteen hundred pornography users, more than half noticed that they needed to watch more extreme or deviant pornographic images in order to orgasm. More than a third of respondents felt ashamed of the kind of pornography they watched. Because escalation and shame are characteristics of all addictions, some researchers claim that this indicates that online pornography is addictive.

Tastes change over time:

64%

Note that their tastes in pornography have become more extreme and/or deviant

36%

Are ashamed about their more extreme/ deviant tastes

Source: "Taking a Whack Out of Porn," Infographic, ProjectKnow.com, 2013. www.projectknow.com.

- According to psychologist Jason Winters, the research that supports sex addiction as a disorder is inconclusive because control groups (people who are not seeking treatment for sex addiction) are never included in research studies.

- Since the 1950s, scientific research has clearly established that those who masturbate have more fulfilling and satisfactory sexual lives. This contradicts the view of sex addiction experts that masturbation can contribute to sex addiction.

- Sex addiction expert Dr. Martin Kafka defines hypersexuality (another term for sex addiction) as having **7 or more orgasms** a week. However, a University of Bristol study of **1,000 men** found that men who had more orgasms in a week lived substantially longer than those who had few or no orgasms.

- Statistics have shown that most people who are diagnosed with sex addiction also have a personality or mood disorder that has hypersexuality as a symptom.

- A 2013 University of California, Los Angeles, study found no difference between the brain activity of individuals diagnosed with sex addiction and those who had a high sex drive but no signs of addiction.

- Research by psychologist Jason Winters found that frequency of sexual activity was not a predictor of sex addiction, but negative religious views about sex were.

Key People and Advocacy Groups

Patrick J. Carnes: A psychologist widely regarded as the father of sexual addiction research who published the seminal work on the subject, *Out of the Shadows: Understanding Sexual Addiction.*

Claire Dines: A professor of sociology, an antipornography activist, and the author of *Pornland: How Porn Has Hijacked Our Sexuality.*

Fight The New Drug (FTND): An education and advocacy group that works to spread the word among teenagers about the dangers of pornography addiction.

Paula Hall: A psychotherapist specializing in sexual addictions who has published widely in academic journals and founded The Hall Recovery Course for sexual addictions.

Marty Klein: A sex therapist, the author of *America's War on Sex*, and a prominent critic of the concept of sexual addiction.

David J. Ley: A clinical psychologist specializing in sexual issues and author of the book *The Myth of Sex Addiction.*

NoFap: A social media support group that helps individuals who want to give up masturbation or pornography.

Stanton Peele: A prominent psychologist in the field of addiction who challenges the sexual addiction recovery movement.

Sex and Love Addicts Anonymous (SLAA): The first 12-step program for sexual addictions, SLAA has a large number of resources available on its website.

The Society for the Advancement of Sexual Health (SASH):
SASH is a membership organization founded by Patrick J. Carnes, dedicated to helping people with sexual addiction problems.

Robert Weiss: A licensed clinical social worker and international sexual addiction expert who founded the Sexual Recovery Institute and has published widely on sexual addiction issues.

Gary Wilson: A sexual addiction educator who hosts the website Your Brain on Porn, a clearinghouse for news and information about sexual addictions.

Chronology

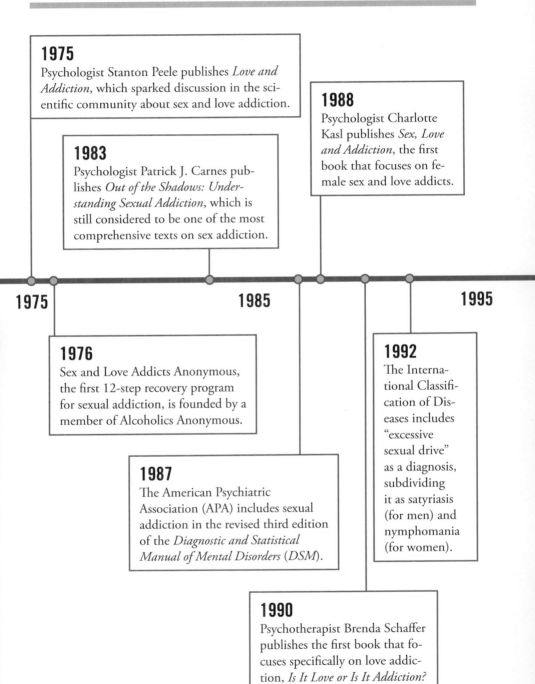

1975
Psychologist Stanton Peele publishes *Love and Addiction*, which sparked discussion in the scientific community about sex and love addiction.

1988
Psychologist Charlotte Kasl publishes *Sex, Love and Addiction*, the first book that focuses on female sex and love addicts.

1983
Psychologist Patrick J. Carnes publishes *Out of the Shadows: Understanding Sexual Addiction*, which is still considered to be one of the most comprehensive texts on sex addiction.

1975　　　　　　　　　1985　　　　　　　　　1995

1976
Sex and Love Addicts Anonymous, the first 12-step recovery program for sexual addiction, is founded by a member of Alcoholics Anonymous.

1992
The International Classification of Diseases includes "excessive sexual drive" as a diagnosis, subdividing it as satyriasis (for men) and nymphomania (for women).

1987
The American Psychiatric Association (APA) includes sexual addiction in the revised third edition of the *Diagnostic and Statistical Manual of Mental Disorders (DSM)*.

1990
Psychotherapist Brenda Schaffer publishes the first book that focuses specifically on love addiction, *Is It Love or Is It Addiction?*

2013
After prolonged debate, the APA does not include sex addiction or hypersexuality as a diagnosis in the *DSM-5*.

2000
The APA removes sexual addiction from the fourth edition of the *DSM*.

2011
The American Society of Addiction Medicine defines all forms of addiction, including behavioral addictions such as sex addiction, as brain diseases.

2008
Actor David Duchovny, who plays a sex addict in the Showtime series *Californication*, enters rehab for sex addiction.

2000

2010

1998
President Bill Clinton has an affair with White House intern Monica Lewinsky. Many pundits in the press accuse Clinton of having a sex addiction.

2009
Professional golfer Tiger Woods enters rehab for sex addiction after being caught having multiple extramarital affairs.

2005
Sex addiction therapist Robert Weiss publishes *Cruise Control*, the first book for gay male sex addicts.

2014
Neuropsychiatrist Valerie Voon conducts the first study that shows that the brains of sex addicts and the brains of substance addicts react in the same way to the objects of their addiction.

Related Organizations

Association for the Treatment of Sexual Addiction and Compulsivity (ATSAC)
PO Box 16486
Birmingham B6 9ED, UK
phone: +44 (0)7414-787341
e-mail: info@atsac.co.uk
website: www.atsac.co.uk

ATSAC is a nonprofit organization in the United Kingdom that provides information and support for sex addiction and recovery. The organization offers a professional certification in sex addiction treatment.

Enough Is Enough
746 Walker Rd., Suite 116
Great Falls, VA 22066
phone: (703) 476-7890
fax: (703) 476-7894
website: www.protectkids.com

Enough Is Enough is a nonprofit organization dedicated to protecting children in cyberspace. Its online resource Protect Kids contains numerous articles about teens and online pornography and youth.

The International Institute for Trauma & Addiction Professionals (IITAP)
PO Box 2112
Carefree, AZ 85377
phone: (866) 575-6853
fax: (480) 595-4753
e-mail: info@iitap.com
website: www.sexhelp.com

Founded by Patrick J. Carnes, IITAP offers training and certification in sex addiction therapy. The organization's website contains educational materials about sex addiction as well as several online screening tests.

The Kinsey Institute

Morrison Hall 302
1165 E. Third St.
Bloomington, IN 47405
phone: (812) 855-7686
fax: (812) 855-8277
e-mail: kinsey@indiana.edu
website: www.kinseyinstitute.org

The Kinsey Institute conducts research to advance sexual health and knowledge about critical issues in sex, gender, and reproduction. The institute is an excellent source of facts and statistics about sexual issues and behavior, including sex addiction and pornography use.

National Institute on Drug Abuse (NIDA)

6001 Executive Blvd., Room 5213
Bethesda, MD 20892-9561
phone: (301) 443-1124
e-mail: webmaster@nida.nih.gov
website: www.drugabuse.gov
teen website: www.teens.drugabuse.gov

NIDA is a federal organization that provides information about substance addictions and advocates using science-based approaches to understanding and treating addiction. While NIDA does not address sexual addictions specifically, it provides a wealth of background information on the principles of addiction. Its companion site NIDA for Teens offers homework help and contains videos and a blog.

Sex Addicts Anonymous (SAA)

PO Box 70949
Houston, TX 77270
phone: (800) 477-8191
e-mail: webmaster@saa-recovery.org
website: https://saa-recovery.org

SAA is one of the few 12-step sex addiction programs that specifically welcomes women and has a large female membership. SAA uses the book

Sex Addicts Anonymous, also known as the Green Book. It is available on its website along with the SA newsletter and other educational information.

Sexaholics Anonymous (SA)

PO Box 3565
Brentwood, TN 37024
phone: (866) 424-8777
fax: (615) 370-0882
e-mail: saico@sa.org
website: www.sa.org

SA is the only 12-step program that defines sexual sobriety for its members as no masturbation or sex outside of marriage. SA uses the book *Sexaholics Anonymous*, also known as the White Book, which is available on its website along with other educational information.

Sex and Love Addicts Anonymous (SLAA)

1550 NE Loop 410, Suite 118
San Antonio, TX 78209
phone: (210) 439-1123
e-mail: info@slaafws.org
website: www.slaafws.org

Created by members of Alcoholics Anonymous in 1976, SLAA was the first 12-step program to address sexual addictions. It is also one of the largest, with over sixteen thousand members and twelve hundred meetings in forty-three countries. SLAA uses the book *Sex and Love Addicts Anonymous*, also known as Basic Text. Its website contains resources and an online store.

Sexual Compulsives Anonymous (SCA)

PO Box 1585
Old Chelsea Station
New York, NY 10011
phone: (212) 828-7900
website: www.sca-recovery.org

SCA was originally formed to address issues of sexual compulsion among gay and bisexual men. It developed its own sexual compulsion screening test called "The Twenty Questions," which is available on its website along with its primary book *Sexual Compulsives Anonymous* and other educational material.

The Sexual Recovery Institute (SRI)

1964 Westwood Blvd., Suite 400
Los Angeles, CA 90025
ph: (877) 959-4114
website: www.sexualrecovery.com

SRI is one of the world's top sex addiction treatment centers. It was founded in 1995 by Robert Weiss, who based its intensive two-week recovery program on the theories of sex addiction developed by Patrick J. Carnes. SRI's website contains a wealth of educational material.

The Society for the Advancement of Sexual Health (SASH)

PO Box 433
Royston, GA 30662
phone: (706) 356-7031
fax: (866) 389-3974
e-mail: sash@sash.net
website: www.sash.net

SASH is dedicated to promoting sexual health by supporting education, scholarship, and research in problematic sexual behaviors such as sex addiction, hypersexual disorder, and sexual abuse. SASH's website contains educational material and links to books and journal articles about sexual addiction.

For Further Research

Books

Patrick J. Carnes, *Out of the Shadows: Understanding Sexual Addiction.* Center City, MN: Hazelden, 1983.

Paula Hall, *Understanding and Treating Sex Addiction.* New York: Routledge, 2013.

Marty Klein, *America's War on Sex.* Santa Barbara, CA: Praeger, 2012.

David J. Ley, *The Myth of Sex Addiction.* Lanham, MD: Rowman & Littlefield, 2012.

Connie A. Lofgreen, *The Storm of Sex Addiction: Rescue and Recovery.* Omaha, NE: Starpro, 2012.

Ogi Ogas and Sai Gaddam, *A Billion Wicked Thoughts: What the World's Largest Experiment Reveals About Human Desire.* New York: Dutton, 2011.

T.C. Ryan, *Ashamed No More: A Pastor's Journal Through Sex Addiction.* Downers Grove, IL: IVP Books, 2012.

Ethlie Ann Vare, *Love Addict: Sex, Romance, and Other Dangerous Drugs.* Deerfield Beach, FL: HCI, 2011.

Robert Weiss, *Cruise Control: Understanding Sex Addiction in Gay Men.* Carefree, AZ: Gentle Path, 2013.

Periodicals

Rachel Pomerance Berl, "Sex Addiction: An Intimacy Disorder," *U.S. News and World Report*, September 30, 2013.

John Cloud, "Sex Addiction: A Disease or a Convenient Excuse?," *Time*, February 28, 2011.

Paula Hall, "A Biopsychosocial View of Sex Addiction," *Sexual and Relationship Therapy*, vol. 26, no. 3, August 2011.

Alexandra Katehakis, "The Link Between Adult Attachment Styles and Sex and Love Addiction," *Psychology Today*, September 5, 2011.

Chris Lee, "The Sex Addiction Epidemic," *Newsweek*, November 29, 2011.

Howard Markel, "The D.S.M. Gets Addiction Right," *New York Times*, June 5, 2012.

David Segal, "Does Porn Hurt Children?," *New York Times*, March 28, 2014.

Alice Walton, "Does Sex Addiction Function Like Drug Addiction in the Brain?," *Forbes*, July 12, 2014.

Kirsten Weir, "Is Pornography Addictive?," *Monitor on Psychology*, April 2014.

Internet Sources

Isaac Abel, "Did Porn Warp Me Forever?," *Salon*, January 12, 2013. www .salon.com/2013/01/13/did_porn_warp_me_forever.

Patrick Carnes, "Sex Addiction 101," IITAP, 2012. www.iitap.com/res ources/training-material/media-presentation.

Martin Daubney, "Experiment That Convinced Me Online Porn Is the Most Pernicious Threat Facing Children Today," *MailOnline*, September 25, 2013. www.dailymail.co.uk/femail/article-2432591 /Porn-pernicious-threat-facing-children-today-By-ex-lads-mag-edi tor-MARTIN-DAUBNEY.html.

Scott Alexander Hess, "The Sex Addict Defense," The Fix, October 7, 2012. www.thefix.com/content/cheating-sex-addiction-Anderson-Cooper-Maisani8520.

Marty Klein, "Are These Symptoms of Sex Addiction? No," *Sexual Intel-ligence* (blog), October 28, 2013. http://sexualintelligence.wordpress .com/2013/10/28/are-these-symptoms-of-sex-addiction-no.

Marty Klein, "You're Addicted to What?," *Humanist*, June 28, 2012. http://thehumanist.com/magazine/july-august-2012/features/youre -addicted-to-what.

Robert Weiss, "Hypersexuality: Symptoms of Sexual Addiction," Psych-Central, 2012. http://psychcentral.com/lib/hypersexuality-sympt oms-of-sexual-addiction/00011488.

Robert Weiss, "Is *Thanks for Sharing* an Honest Look Inside Sex Addic-tion Recovery?," *Huffington Post*, September 24, 2013. www.huffing tonpost.com/robert-weiss/thanks-for-sharing-review_b_3982933 .html.

Source Notes

Overview

1. Marty Klein, interview by Dan Savage, "Savage Lovecast Episode 326," podcast, Savage Lovecast, January 22, 2013. www.savagelovecast.com.
2. Quoted in John Cloud, "Sex Addiction: A Disease or a Convenient Excuse?," *Time*, February 28, 2011. http://content.time.com.
3. Quoted in Cloud, "Sex Addiction: A Disease or a Convenient Excuse?"
4. David Linden, interview by Terry Gross, "'Compass of Pleasure': Why Some Things Feel So Good," *Fresh Air*, NPR, June 23, 2011. www.npr.org.
5. Robert Weiss, "Information for Sex Addicts," Robert Weiss MSW, 2014. www.robertweissmsw.com.
6. Calum, interview by Martin Daubney, *Porn on the Brain*, Channel 4 (UK television network), September 30, 2013. www.channel4.com.
7. Isaac Abel, "Did Porn Warp Me Forever?," *Salon*, January 12, 2013. www.salon.com.
8. Quoted in Laura Barnett, "Shame: Sex Addicts Reveal All," *Guardian*, January 10, 2012. www.theguardian.com.
9. Weiss, "Information for Sex Addicts."
10. Sexaholics Anonymous, "What Is a Sexaholic and What Is Sexual Sobriety?," 2001. www.sa.org.
11. Marty Klein, "You're Addicted to What?," *Humanist*, June 28, 2012. http://thehumanist.com.
12. Klein, "You're Addicted to What?"

What Is Sex Addiction?

13. Patrick J. Carnes, "The Making of a Sex Addict," (adapted from Patrick J. Carnes, "The Obsessive Shadow," 1998), International Institute for Trauma and Addiction, 2008. www.iitap.com.
14. Paula Hall, "A Biopsychosocial View of Sex Addiction," *Sexual and Relationship Therapy*, vol. 26, no. 3, August 2011, p. 218.
15. Alexandra Katehakis, "The Link Between Adult Attachment Styles and Sex and Love Addiction," *Psychology Today* (blog), September 5, 2011. www.psychologytoday.com.
16. Stanton Peele, "Addiction in Society: Blinded by Biochemistry," *Psychology Today*, June 15, 2011. www.psychologytoday.com.
17. Robert Weiss, "Hypersexuality: Symptoms of Sexual Addiction," PsychCentral, 2012. http://psychcentral.com.
18. Gary Wilson, *The Great Porn Experiment*, video, TEDxGlasgow, YouTube, May 16, 2012. www.youtube.com.
19. Robert Weiss, "The Clinical Assessment and Treatment of Sex and Porn Addiction," SlidePlayer, 2011. http://slideplayer.us.
20. Quoted in Barnett, "Shame: Sex Addicts Reveal All."

21. Quoted in Sue William Silverman, *Love Sick: One Woman's Journey Through Sexual Addiction*, Kindle edition. New York: W.W. Norton, 2001.
22. Moushumi Ghose, "Addicted to Love: Drawn to the Rush of Romance," Good Therapy.org, November 2, 2012. www.goodtherapy.org.
23. Quoted in Barnett, "Shame: Sex Addicts Reveal All."
24. Paula Hall, *Understanding and Treating Sex Addiction*, Kindle edition. New York: Routledge, 2013.

What Is Pornography Addiction?

25. Nathan Haug, interview, "The Teenage Brain on Porn," ABC *Nightline*, October 31, 2013. www.hulu.com.
26. Patrick J. Carnes, interview, "Sexual Addiction Interview with Dr. Patrick Carnes," Pine Grove Behavioral Health and Addiction Services, March 13, 2014. www.pine grovetreatment.com.
27. Wilson, *The Great Porn Experiment*.
28. Jesse Bering, "Dear Jesse, I'm an Atheistic Porn Addict," *Bering in Mind* (blog), *Scientific American*, January 23, 2012. http://blogs.scientificamerican.com.
29. Fight The New Drug, "Get the Facts." www.fightthenewdrug.org.
30. Quoted in Fight The New Drug, "Get the Facts."
31. Gary Wilson, "Without the Coolidge Effect There Would Be No Internet Porn," Your Brain on Porn, August 8, 2011. http://yourbrainonporn.com.
32. Gail Dines, *Pornland*, Kindle edition. Boston: Beacon, 2010.
33. Fight The New Drug, "Get the Facts."
34. Dines, *Pornland*.
35. Matt Field, interview by Martin Daubney, *Porn on the Brain*, Channel 4 (UK television network).
36. Paul J. Wright and Ashley K. Randall, "Internet Pornography Exposure and Risky Sexual Behavior Among Adult Males in the United States," *Computers in Human Behavior*, April 1, 2012, p. 1413.
37. Breanne Saldivar, interview by Martin Daubney, *Porn on the Brain*, Channel 4 (UK television network).
38. Janie Lacy, "Five Reasons Porn Can Hurt Your Love Life," GoodTherapy.org, January 9, 2013. www.goodtherapy.org.
39. Calum, interview by Martin Daubney, *Porn on the Brain*, Channel 4 (UK television network).
40. Dines, *Pornland*.
41. Abel, "Did Porn Warp Me Forever?"
42. Abel, "Did Porn Warp Me Forever?"

Can Sex and Pornography Addictions Be Overcome?

43. Robert Weiss, "Is *Thanks for Sharing* an Honest Look Inside Sex Addiction Recovery?," *Huffington Post*, September 24, 2013. www.huffingtonpost.com.
44. AAMFT, "AAMFT Therapy Topic: Sexual Addiction." www.aamft.org.
45. Sexaholics Anonymous, "What Is a Sexaholic and What Is Sexual Sobriety?" www.sa.org/sexaholic.php.

46. Quoted in Chris Lee, "The Sex Addiction Epidemic," *Newsweek*, November 29, 2011. www.newsweek.com.
47. Quoted in Daily Beast, "Eight Facts About Sex Rehab," June 15, 2011. www.thedaily beast.com.
48. Johnny Hunt, interview by Martin Daubney, *Porn on the Brain*, Channel 4 (UK television network).
49. Dines, *Pornland.*
50. Amy Danahay, interview by Martin Daubney, *Porn on the Brain*, Channel 4 (UK television network).
51. Respect Yourself, "I'm Addicted to Porn and It Turns Me On but . . . ." www.respect yourself.info.

Are Sex and Pornography Really Addictive?

52. Klein, "You're Addicted to What?"
53. Klein, "You're Addicted to What?"
54. David J. Ley, *The Myth of Sex Addiction*, Kindle edition. Lanham, MD: Rowman & Littlefield, 2012.
55. National Institute on Drug Abuse, "The Science of Drug Abuse and Addiction," December 2012. www.drugabuse.gov.
56. Klein, "You're Addicted to What?"
57. Klein, "You're Addicted to What?"
58. Allen Frances, "DSM-5 Is a Guide, Not a Bible—Simply Ignore Its 10 Worst Changes," *Psychiatric Times*, December 4, 2012. www.psychiatrictimes.com.
59. Peele, "Addiction in Society: Blinded by Biochemistry."
60. Peele, "Addiction in Society: Blinded by Biochemistry."
61. Sex Addicts Anonymous, "The Twelve Steps." https://saa-recovery.org.
62. *Thanks for Sharing,* movie, directed by Stuart Blumberg, Lionsgate, 2012.
63. Ley, *The Myth of Sex Addiction.*
64. Klein, "You're Addicted to What?"
65. Weiss, "Information for Sex Addicts."
66. Patrick J. Carnes, "Sexual Addiction Screening Test—Revised," Foundry Clinical Group. http://foundryclinicalgroup.com.
67. Quoted in Ley, *The Myth of Sex Addiction.*
68. Carnes, "Sexual Addiction Screening Test—Revised."
69. Quoted in Stephanie Pappas, "Bondage Benefits: BDSM Practitioners Healthier than 'Vanilla' People," livescience, May 29, 2013. www.livescience.com.
70. Quoted in David J. Ley, "The Profit in Sex Addiction," *Psychology Today*, November 16, 2011. www.psychologytoday.com.
71. Ley, "The Profit in Sex Addiction."
72. Quoted in Scott Alexander Hess, "The Sex Addict Defense," The Fix, October 7, 2012. www.thefix.com.

List of Illustrations

What Is Sex Addiction?

The Sexual Activities of Sex Addicts	32
Sex Addicts Usually Have Other Addictions	33
The Cycle of Sex Addiction	34

What Is Pornography Addiction?

The Male Sex Drive Is Novelty Seeking	46
Women More Concerned About Partners' Porn Use than Men	47
Women Believe Porn Interferes with Sex	48

Can Sex and Pornography Addictions Be Overcome?

Benefits of Abstaining from Pornography and Masturbation	60
Identifying Triggers	61
Parent-Child Communication and Porn Use	62

Are Sex and Pornography Really Addictive?

Many People Say Sex Addiction Is Not a Medical Condition	75
Over Time, Tastes in Porn Become More Extreme	76

Index

Note: Boldface page numbers indicate illustrations.

Abel, Isaac, 41
addiction(s)
  coexisting with sex/pornography addiction, 66
    prevalence of, 32, **33**
  debate on whether sex/pornography can cause, 19–20, 63, 64–65
  rewiring of brain and, 64
  as self-soothing mechanism, 23
  See also specific types
alternative sexuality, 68–69
American Association for Marriage and Family Therapy, 50
American Association of Christian Counselors, 19
American Psychological Association (APA), 14, 23, 65, 74
attachment disorders, 8, 22–23, 61

Bering, Jesse, 36, 72
brain
  addiction and, 19–20, 64–65
  behavioral addictions and, 65
Brand, Russell, 53

Carnes, Patrick J., 20, 33, 36, 64
  on history of childhood trauma among sex addicts, 21–22
  on length of time required to overcome sex addiction, 62
  on sex addiction and suicide, 30, 59
  on types of sex addiction, 17–18
child abuse/trauma

  as cause of sexual addiction, 8, 21–22, 66
  prevalence of sex addicts being victims of, 13
  triggers for sexual addiction and, 51–52, **61**
child molestation, percentage of people convicted meeting criteria for sex addiction, 31
child pornography, 38
Christian Recovery movement, 52
Cognitive Behavioral Therapy (CBT), 54
Collins, Barry, 57
Computers in Human Behavior (journal), 39
Coolidge Effect, 46
CovenantEyes, 45, 46

Danahay, Amy, 55, 58
Daubney, Martin, 13, 35, 44
Denton, Jill, 43
Diagnostic and Statistical Manual of Mental Disorders (DSM), 10, 20
  introduction of behavioral addictions in, 65
Dines, Gail, 38, 41, 44, 55
dopamine, 29, 37, 38, 40, 64
Duchovny, David, 53, 62

Field, Matt, 39
Fight The New Drug (FTND), 36–37, 38, 54–55
filtering software, 57
Fischer, Jessi, 63
Frances, Allen, 65, 72

Gaddam, Sai, 45, 72

gambling addiction, 20, 65

Ghose, Moushumi, 21, 27, 29, 43

gonzo porn, 38

Grant, Jon E., 58

Hall, Paula, 10, 29, 30, 71
- on age of onset of sexual addiction, 31
- on celebacy/abstinence from masturbation, 57
- on childhood trauma and sex addiction, 22
- on shame associated with sex addiction, 27

Haug, Nathan, 35

Hayden, Dorothy, 56

Herkov, Michael, 31

Hunt, Johnny, 44, 55

hypersexual disorder, 18

hypersexuality, definition of, 77

infidelity
- associated with pornography viewing, 48
- sex addiction and, 66, 69

International Institute for Trauma and Addiction Professionals (IITAP), 49, 54

Journal of Sexual Medicine, 68

Kafka, Martin, 77

Katehakis, Alexandra, 22, 69

Klein, Marty, 11, 49
- on diagnosis of sex addiction, 10, 63, 72
- on problem with sex addiction treatment programs, 57
- on sex addiction and narcissism, 20

Lacy, Janie, 28, 29, 40, 43

Ley, David J., 43, 56, 71
- on danger of sex addiction label, 28, 73
- on Internet pornography and sex crimes, 42
- on prevalence of mental illness in people seeking sex addiction treatment, 60
- on 12-step programs, 66

Linden, David, 12–13

Lofgreen, Connie A., 29

love addiction, 24, 26–27, 29

masturbation
- benefits of abstaining from, **60**
- research showing benefits of, 76

Melincovich, Neil, 10, 11

mental disorders
- hypersexuality as symptom of, 77
- prevalence among people seeking sex addiction treatment, 60
- survey on views of, as medical conditions, **75**

Meyer, Cathy, 69–70

mood disorders, accompanying sex/pornography addictions, 9

narcissism/narcissistic personalities, 20, 23

National Institute on Drug Abuse (NIDA), 64

NoFap (social media group), 19, 45, 52–53, 59

nonmonogamy, consensual, 67–68

Ogas, Ogi, 45, 72

opinion polls. *See* surveys

Out of the Shadows (Carnes), 20

Peele, Stanton, 23, 65

personality disorders, 13
- accompanying sex/pornography addictions, 9, 23–24

polls. *See* surveys
porn-induced erectile dysfunction
    (PIED), 40–41
Pornland (Dines), 55
pornography
    benefits of abstaining from, **60**
    compulsive behavior and, 37–38
    as gateway to sex addiction, 39
    prevalence on Internet, 45
    risk of committing sexual offenses
        among people viewing, 60
pornography addiction
    causes of, 8, 36–37
    controversy over, 19–20
    definition of, 8, 13–14
    as harmful to relationships, 40
    impact on sexual responses, 41
    prevalence of, 9, 17, 39
    prevention of, 54–55
    signs of, 14–16
    See also treatment
powerlessness, 56
    in addiction *vs.* therapy models, 73
    as concept in 12-step programs,
        65–66
pregnancies, unplanned, among
    female sex addicts, 59

research
    on pornography addiction,
        difficulties with, 36
    on sex addiction
        is anecdotal, 21
        is inconclusive, 76
Respect Yourself (website), 45

Saldivar, Breanne, 40
Satinover, Jeffrey, 37
Savage, Dan, 38, 67
sex addiction
    addictions coexisting with, 32
        prevalence of, **33**

age of onset of, 31
causes of, 8
controversy over, 19–20
critics of concept of, 67–69
cycle of, 24–25, **34**
definition of, 8, 11–13, 67
harmful affects of, 27
intimacy problems and, 13
prevalence of, 9, 17, 31
    gender differences in, 31
sexual fetishes *vs.,* 16–17
shame associated with, 27, 29
signs of, 14–16
stigma associated with diagnosis
    of, 28
triggers for, **61**
types of, 17–18
See also treatment
Sex Addiction Therapist
    certification for, 59
    lack of research showing
        effectiveness of, 74
Sex Addicts Anonymous (SAA), 10,
    50
Sexaholics Anonymous (SA), 19, 51
sex drive, male, as novelty seeking, **46**
Sexual Addiction & Compulsivity
    (journal), 23, 32, 48
Sexual Addiction Screening Test
    (SAST), 14, 67, 68
sexual anorexia, 18
sexual fetishes, 16–17
sexuality, alternative, 68–69
sexual offenses
    incidences have dropped since
        advent of Internet, 74
    Internet pornography and, 42
    risk of committing, among people
        viewing pornography, 60
Sexual Recovery Institute, 32, 51
Social Science Quarterly (journal), 48
Sophy, Charles, 53

suicide, sex addiction and, 59

surveys
  of adolescents, on viewing online pornography/discussions with parents about, **62**
  on aggressive content in online pornography, 47
  on characteristics of sex addicts, 31
  of concerns of men *vs.* women on partners' use of pornography, **47**
  on male college students' use of pornographic websites, 45
  of pornography users on need for more extreme/deviant porn, **76**
  on prevalence of personality disorders in men seeking help for sex addiction, 23
  on sexual activities engaged in by sex addicts, **32**
  on types of pornography viewed by children, 46
  on unplanned pregnancies among female sex addicts, 59
  on views of mental health issues as medical conditions, **75**
  of women on pornography interfering with sex, **48**

Thanks for Sharing (film), 49, 51, 66
Time (magazine), 50
tolerance
  in drug *vs.* sex addiction, 15
  to pornography, 14
    chemical basis of, 38
treatment, 9, 10
  from Christian perspective, 19, 52
  cost of, 69
    for residential programs, 59
  online programs, 52–53

outpatient therapy, 54
profit motive and, 69–70
through 12-step programs, 18–19, 49, 50–51, 59
"Triple A Engine" effect, 36
Tru Research, 45
12-step programs, 49, 50–51, 59
  notion of powerlessness in, 65–66

Violence Against Women (journal), *47*
Voon, Valerie, 63, 64
Vrangalova, Zhana, 68

Weiss, Robert, 49, 51, 64
  on definition of sex addiction, 13
  on filtering software, 57
  on prevalence of females seeking treatment for sex addiction, 31
  on risks of sex addiction, 21
  on stages of sexual addiction cycle, 24–25
Wilson, Gary, 24, 36, 37–38
Winters, Jason, 76, 77
Wismeijer, Andreas, 68
withdrawal, 15
Woods, John, 42
Woods, Tiger, 53

XXXChurch.com (website), 52

YouPorn (website), 45
youth
  dangers of pornography to, 9
  percentages viewing online pornography/having discussions with parents about, **62**
  prevalence of pornography viewing among, 46

About the Author

Christine Wilcox writes fiction and nonfiction for young adults and adults. She has worked as an editor, an instructional designer, and a writing instructor. She lives in Richmond, Virginia, with her husband, David, and her son, Doug.